BREAKING

Generational

CURSES

Releasing God's Power in Us, Our Children, and Our Destiny

DON NORI

Destiny Image₍ᵣ₎ Publishers, Inc.

P.O. Box 310
Shippensburg, PA 17257-0310

"We Publish the Prophets"

Previously Published ISBN 0-7684-2037-7
Revised Edition ISBN: 0-7684-2282-5

For Worldwide Distribution
Printed in the U.S.A.

This book and all other Destiny Image, Revival Press, and Treasure House books are available at Christian bookstores and distributors worldwide.

Call toll free:
1-800-722-6774.

For more information on foreign distributors, call
717-532-3040.

Or reach us on the Internet:
www.destinyimage.com

DEDICATION

The principles of this book were discovered in God's Word, but they were forged into our hearts over many years of struggle, search, and commitment.

There is one whose heart has taught me more about unconditional love and daily, loving commitment to children than a hundred Bible studies could ever have taught me. Her passionate intercessory prayer, her tenacious resolve, and her constant unselfishness have made our family what it is today.

To Cathy, my wife of more than 32 years, I dedicate this book.

ENDORSEMENT

"If you believe that your ministry can be fulfilled in one generation, then your vision of God is too small. Our God is the God of Abraham, Isaac, and Jacob. The blessing of previous generations must be passed down to the next generation or Kingdom manifestation will be contained in momentary outpourings limited by time and space. For the entire earth to be filled with the glory of God, we must understand that our harvest will never be greater than our seed. A father must understand that his greatest ministry is bequeathed in sons and daughters who bridge the gap of generational inheritance in the Spirit. My friend, Don Nori, has lived this truth and now shares it with you."

—Dr. Mark Hanby
Apostle, Author, Speaker

TABLE OF CONTENTS

INTRODUCTION

Our future is not just in Heaven; it is also in our loins. Christians are beginning to realize that we have a powerful biblical mandate to prepare our sons and daughters to carry the torch of His Presence into the decades ahead of us. If the Kingdom of God is to advance from generation to generation, there must be a radical change in our attitudes toward our children. We must understand that the church He is building is not built with bricks and mortar. It is established in the hearts of our children as we teach them by word and example to yield to the will of God. I want to hand my children the flaming torch of His Presence so they may go forward from where I gave them the torch. I do not want them to have to start at the beginning, re-learning the hard lessons of life that I struggled so hard to learn. I can give them a jump start by pouring all I am into their hearts and lives.

I am not interested in preparing any of my five sons for anything less than God's plan for their lives in the Kingdom of God. My goal and my passion is to see my children grow up to not merely accept my faith passively, but to aggressively and passionately pursue the Lord. I want my sons to know that true fulfillment comes through joyfully doing the will of God. To that end, I give myself to them as much as I feel I need to, not as much as I feel I can. For if I were to respond to my children according to the demands that are on my schedule, I would spend very little time with them. So my priorities have changed over the years. I have put their needs before mine, before the things that constantly scream for my attention.

In the years to come, when we all look back over our past, wondering where the years have gone, we will look for meaning. We will wonder what will really last of what we have done. When I reach that point of reflection in my life, I will point to my sons and declare that my years were not wasted, for they are captured in the lives of my sons. Where have my years gone? They have gone into the hearts of my children. Not one minute has fallen to the ground. My history, my life, my love and abilities are safely tucked within the lives of my sons, whom I have loved and cherished these many years.

My ability to affect the generations to come has very little to do with what I build or how many people were in my church. It has nothing to do with how many books I have written or how many videotapes I have made. These things do not contain and cannot hold a man's anointing. This anointing can be contained only by his seed.

Parents who have a passion for the Church of the next century need to begin to pour their love, attention, time, and instruction into their children, knowing that something wonderful happens in this process. God takes that substance of spirit that He has carefully formed in you with instruction and training and somehow pours it into the little ones He has entrusted to you.

Our children have a mighty opportunity to carry our legacy and our anointing to places where we will never be able to go and to years far into the next century—and through their children, far beyond even them. Let us look again at our priorities. Let us understand that our future is as secure as we have formed our children into vessels prepared to carry that which God poured into us from the generations before us.

It is my prayer that the pages of this book will ignite in you a passion and a resolve for your children to hear and respond to the plan God has had in His heart for the generations. May the words you read on these pages cause you to understand that all God has given you will not go to the grave with you, but will live on in the lives of your children, their children, and their children's children's children.

PART ONE

GOD LOVES THE GENERATIONS

One generation will commend Your works to another; they will tell of Your mighty acts. They will speak of the glorious splendor of Your majesty, and I will meditate on Your wonderful works. They will tell of the power of Your awesome works, and I will proclaim Your great deeds.... They will tell of the glory of Your kingdom and speak of Your might, so that all men may know of Your mighty acts and the glorious splendor of Your kingdom. Your kingdom is an everlasting kingdom, and Your dominion endures through all generations. The Lord is faithful to all His promises and loving toward all He has made (Psalm 145:4-6,11-13).

CHAPTER ONE

Touching Your Children's Children's Children

A lonely beggar lay drunk and shivering in the muddy slime of a drainage ditch in Peking, China. Throughout the night hours, as he grew closer to death, the beggar's plight went either unnoticed or ignored by the few passersby. Finally, as darkness gave way to the light of dawn, a stranger saw him and reached out in compassion. After gently lifting the cold and broken frame of the man out of the ditch, the stranger took him into his own home. The beggar was nursed back to health as the compassionate stranger told him of the Savior who had come to this world to pull lost souls out of the pit of despair and eternal darkness; a Savior who came to give abundant life. The beggar turned his life over to Jesus Christ and went on to become China's first national preacher of the gospel.

FIVE *Generations* LATER

Five generations later I sat and listened to that beggar's great-great-great-grandson tell the story of how the Lord had brought salvation to his family through that miraculous intervention in Peking. The grandson told me that in every generation since, his family members have been missionaries, pastors, and evangelists. My young friend, who himself was a missionary from China to America, gave the wonderful testimony of how a stranger had pulled his great-great-great-grandfather from a ditch and set his life on a whole new course.

The stranger's name was Hudson Taylor.

Until the day he was pulled out of the ditch, my young friend's great-great-great-grandfather, who had come from a long line of thieves and vagabonds, lived his life the way his family had for many years.

I wonder if it ever crossed Hudson Taylor's mind that in rescuing one man, he was actually saving many generations. If he could have looked into the future, Hudson Taylor would have seen that his one act of kindness changed the destiny of an entire family for generations to come. They were transformed from a family who bequeathed an inheritance of emptiness, into one that possessed and passed on new life and the purposes of God.

GOD *Loves* THE GENERATIONS

The word *generations* is mentioned more than 700 times in Scripture. God is a generational God. Some of us tend to think that the Lord was born three days before we got saved and His purposes are going to be wrapped up about a week after we go to be with Him. As a result, we do not take time to reflect on our past or to hope for our future. We rarely consider people like Hudson Taylor, who served God years ago, and the sacrifices they made that paved the road on which we travel today. We have little awareness of how the blood of martyrs and the suffering of so many believers throughout the ages have preserved the torch of God's Presence so that we, too, may walk with Him.

Neither have we recognized how *our* actions, *our* hopes, and *our* dreams affect the generations to come. Whether we are aware of the fact or not, our lives influence the children around us—the children in our family, the children in our church fellowship, and the children in our neighborhoods. We carry the glorious torch of God's Presence.

In His Word there are 1,314 passages of Scripture that speak about parents and children. Concerning a father's relationship to his son, there are 2,208 verses; and there are 1,426 passages that have instructions to fathers. The portions of Scripture that deal with passing the torch from one generation to the next number 180. It seems obvious that God is interested in having His plan remain in the center of the attention of mankind, from generation to generation.

God is passionate for the preservation of His mercy and righteousness throughout the ages. He sees the whole picture, from beginning to end, and the Lord wants a people who will live not just for themselves, but who will pour themselves into children. He is looking for Christians who will give themselves to equipping and preparing the next generation.

TRAINING *by* EXAMPLE

The lives of children are intended to be primarily molded by what they experience at home. There is a truly spiritual connection between children and their parents. God made it that way. He ordained that youngsters be influenced, trained, and shaped by their mothers and fathers. Children will follow us and will pattern themselves according to the model we set.

Throughout the years in our home, Cathy and I have often noticed how our sons wanted to be wherever we were, doing whatever we were doing. If I was in the family room watching television, they would be cuddled up beside me. If I shut off the TV and picked up a book, that is what they would do. If I was reading my Bible, there were our sons, spread out around the room, reading their Bibles.

The behavior and lifestyle we model to our children will have the strongest impact on who they become. Parents' influence in the home will absolutely overpower the influences on our children at school; it will nullify the most deliberate secular brainwashing. Children were constructed by God with their hearts open to their parents. They learn from us first. If we live a mediocre life of religious activity, it will show in our children. On the other hand, it will also be evident if our spiritual life is wholesome and vibrant with God's life, love, and power.

BUILDING CHURCHES WITH A *Generational* ATTITUDE

"How many people are in your church?" is a frequently asked question; and the common response goes something like this, "We have about 200 adults...plus the children." The next time you are asked that question, I challenge you to give an uncommon response, which might be: "Oh, we have 85 children...plus the adults."

We make children second-class citizens instead of understanding that they are the ones who will carry the torch of God's Presence into the future. If we recognized what is in us, and if we really understood what will die if we don't transfer it, our lives and our ministries would be much different than they are.

KEEP AN EYE *Toward* THE FUTURE

There is something mighty in our children. Our sons and daughters have a call and a purpose. God has dreamed a dream for each one and has written that child's name on that dream. If we will train our children from the womb to understand that God has a destiny for their lives, the result will be confident young people who know who they are. Once we recognize how our present decisions affect our children's future, we will find that we use a lot more caution and wisdom in our daily lives.

People in Third World countries understand this concept much better than we Westerners do. A friend of mine, a Third World Christian pastor, was swindled out of $5,000 by another pastor. I asked my friend, "Well, are you going to just let this go? What are you going to do?" His quiet response was, "I will do nothing. One day my son may need his son. I can't risk a breach of relationship. A dispute like that could possibly prevent my son from getting the help he may need later in his life."

That man is living with a generational mentality. The relationships he makes, the friendships he maintains, the business agreements he signs—all the things he does each day—are done with an eye toward his children and how his decisions will affect their future.

Hezekiah Didn't "Get It" *(But His Children Did)*

Hezekiah was a king who didn't understand the essence of the generations. Isaiah 38 tells how King Hezekiah became very sick. The prophet came and said to him, "Get your house in order, Hezekiah; you are about to die."[1] When the prophet left, Hezekiah rolled over on his bed and cried out to God. His crying and repentance were so sincere that the Lord said to the prophet, "Go back and say to Hezekiah, 'I have heard your words. I have heard your crying. I have heard your repentance, and behold, I'm going to give you another 15 years.' "[2] Later, God said, "Tell Hezekiah that the calamity that I promised to happen now will not happen until he dies. He will not have to face the calamity, *only his children will.*"[3]

Countless sermons have been preached about Hezekiah's great prayer of repentance. Preachers have declared the wonderful fact that Hezekiah cried out to God and the Lord gave him another 15 years.

I don't think Hezekiah was wonderful. He was selfish and self-centered. Did he turn his face to the wall and cry out to God with the same intensity for his children as he had when *his* life was in jeopardy? No, he did not. " 'The word of the Lord you have spoken is *good*,' Hezekiah replied. For he thought, 'There will be peace and security in my lifetime.' "[4]

"The word of the Lord you have spoken is good"?! What was good about it?! In Hezekiah's shallow self-centeredness, it was enough for him that he would live and the enemy would not attack during his lifetime. It was all right for calamity and war to fall onto his children. "Bless God; thank You, Jesus; I live." End of prayer. Hezekiah didn't seem to care that the calamities would fall upon his children instead of himself. His response indicated that he was happy as long as he could live out his life in peace. Oh that Hezekiah would have cried out even more emphatically for his children, "Lord, You have spared me. Now spare my children and their children unto the fourth generation."

As fathers cry out to God, judgment is put off another generation. When their sons rise up and cry out to God, judgment is put off yet another generation. But even praying for the next generation will not suffice if we do not give ourselves to their nurturing, to love, and to daily instruction in living for the Lord.

YOUR MOST *Important* MINISTRY

You mothers and fathers who recognize the value of training your children should be commended. Right now you may not see the strength you are putting into those little people, but God sees it. He watches the mountains of right-eousness you are raising and beholds who your sons and daughters are becoming.

So take heart! When you cannot see beyond the mountains of laundry, the stacks of bills, and the trails of dirt your children have tracked into the house, God sees His calling on your children's lives. He knows that the fruit of your labor—the hours of driving your children to practice and of making sure that they finish their homework—is growing life and love in your child, even though it is not evident to you now. He sees the glory you are planting in them, even if you can't. So let this Scripture encourage you: *"The Kingdom of God does not come with observation"!*[5]

God has entrusted your children to you for a season to raise them for His purposes. The hours you spend working, teaching, training, and praying are priceless; only God knows what that work is producing. Your children will affect the world. They will be men and women who will touch kings and change nations. Do not be discouraged by the time and effort you are putting into raising your sons and daughters. Don't listen to the lies of the enemy that try to steal your crown by saying you are wasting your time when you lovingly and gently give of yourself to your children.

When our sons were small, I was both a businessman and a pastor. The demands on my time were extraordinary. I could easily have been out of my house every night of the week and all weekend. Instead, every night at six o'clock, with piles of work screaming at me to stay at the office, I would lock my office door and go home. My wife and five little people were waiting for me, and I knew that my first responsibility was to them. I was well aware of the impact my presence had on them, and how much my words of encouragement meant.

Parents, your most important ministry is at home. Your children need you. Your words and actions in your home have eternal significance.

Words ARE POWERFUL

Children's earliest opinions of themselves are formed by the words we say to them. Far too often parents speak from their own pain and anger. They say to their children the same hurtful words that their own parents spoke to them.

How many mothers or fathers have been heard to say in July or August, "I can't wait until we can get these 'darn kids' back to school"? Then those parents wonder why their "darn kids" grow up in trouble.

"Oh no, the little hellions are home and that means my day ends. I can't get anything done when they're around!" Parents often say this kind of thing in jest, but children don't take it as a joke. What do children think? "I'm a hellion. I'm always causing trouble. I guess I'll just stay in my room so I'm not in their way. I'll stay out with my friends so I won't bother my parents."

I know a mother who always said that her kids were pests. "You're a pest. You're a pest!" The children heard that so often throughout their childhood that it became ingrained in them. Today they are grown up, but they still hang around their parents' house, hoping and wishing for some positive affirmation, which they still don't receive.

Our children were never, and are not now, pests! We love them and want them around us. They can talk to us as much as they want, and we will listen. There will be a day when we beg God to let them pester us, but they'll be gone. Let's use the precious, fleeting childhood days to pour love and affirmation into our children; to fill them up with words of the hope and destiny they have in God. Let's take the time to listen to them and to let them know how valuable they are to us.

I remember with fondness and an aching heart all the late night conversations Cathy and I had with our sons as they got older. There is something within teenagers that likes the wee hours of the morning. I can't begin to count the number of times when Cathy and I would be so very tired, and one of our sons would want to talk. Many nights we would stay up with them until two or three o'clock in the morning, even on school nights. Sometimes what they wanted to talk about didn't seem that important to us, but we could sense that they were reaching out. There was a need to touch us, a desire to communicate. Cathy and I would stay up as long as they wanted. Our sons are intensely valuable to Cathy and I. That their connection with us stays strong is more important than what they will learn in school the next day. We never wanted our sons to feel that we were too tired or too busy for them. We still try to always give them the attention they need.

Sometimes when they reached out we had to postpone their time with us because we were in the middle of something else. We would say, "Listen, give me one hour to finish this, and then we'll spend as much time as you want." One hour later, to the minute, they would be back, ready to talk. Even if we weren't done with what we had been working on, we would put it aside and give them our full attention.

Time goes by whether we want it to or not. Children do not stay little forever. One day they will be grown-ups, but right now we have the wonderful privilege of pouring into their lives and affecting their future. Let's raise our sons and daughters to be sensitive, Spirit-filled, God-listening people. Let's teach them to pray and live with passion toward the Lord.

Remember: You have a destiny that carries the torch of God's Presence from the past generation, through your generation, and into the next generation. One day the carrying of that torch will be handed on to your children. That is your lifetime responsibility and opportunity, challenge and joy.

ENDNOTES

1. See Isaiah 38:1.
2. See Isaiah 38:5.
3. See Isaiah 39:5-7.
4. Isaiah 39:8.
5. See Luke 17:20b.

Live a generational lifestyle.
The direction you travel today
will pave the way for your children's
journey tomorrow.

---∞---

For God, who said, "Let there be light in the darkness," has made us understand that this light is the brightness of the glory of God that is seen in the face of Jesus Christ. But **this precious treasure—this light and power that now shine within us—is held in perishable containers, that is, in our weak bodies.** *So everyone can see that our glorious power is from God and is not our own* (2 Corinthians 4:6-7 NLT).

---∞---

CHAPTER TWO

Rivers
of
God's Presence

We are carriers of the glory of God. We bear in our bodies the torch of His Presence. God yearns for us to pass on that light to the next generation; He longs for the whole earth to be filled with the glory of the Lord. He is not satisfied with our ability to preach, prophecy, publish books, or write songs. Nor is He gratified by our success in accumulating wealth or making a big name for ourselves. Father God will be content only when we have prepared a vessel to receive the anointing that He has poured into us so that one generation can declare and carry His greatness to the next.[1]

My dad was so proud when our first son, Jonathan, was born. Dad wanted so much for the Nori name to continue. "It's a good name," he would say. "It was clean and respected when my father gave it to me, and it is still clean and respected as I give it to you." My twin brother, Ron, and I didn't understand what he meant years ago, but my dad was certain there had to be many Nori sons to carry forth our name, and its honor had to be kept pure.

As Cathy and I had Don Jr., Matthew, Joel, and Stephan, my dad was as happy as could be. If I were to tell a very private personal belief, I would say that my father was responsible for praying five sons into our family!

Little did we know then, and little do we know now, how our sons will affect the world with the power of the gospel, but we are certain that Granddad Nori will have had a lot to do with it. His need for a strong posterity resulted in the five young and powerful sons we have today.

In the heart of every father is the desire for his name to be carried on. A genuine father wants to perpetuate who he is. This same motivation is also within the hearts of mothers. Parents want to pass on to their children all they have learned in the proverbial school of hard knocks, as well as all that they have built and established. They want every good thing that is within them to pass to their children. Father God has that same longing.

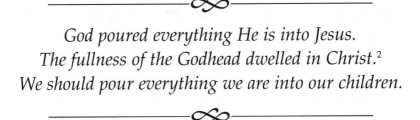

God poured everything He is into Jesus.
The fullness of the Godhead dwelled in Christ.[2]
We should pour everything we are into our children.

A SUSTAINED *Move* OF GOD *Throughout* THE AGES

Rarely has there been a sustained move of God from one generation to the next. History reveals that most revivals have lasted but a few years because God's people became satisfied with what they had received from the Lord, satisfied with the particular way in which He had visited them. This pattern has yet to be broken. Christians too easily become introverted and infatuated with their own giftings and abilities, and the result is that the next generation suffers.

That which the Lord has planted in you and in me brings the earth one step closer to His ultimate purpose. When, however, we fail to pass on to our children all that God poured into us, our children are forced to start over at the beginning. They are forced to plow the same ground and plant the same fields as their fathers. But no more! What God is doing in the earth today must not die with us! We must impart it to our children.

From *Glory* to *Glory*

We are being transformed from one degree of glory to the next.[3] This applies not only to individuals, but to the Church as a whole. We are to be elevated from one place of glory within—which is then passed on to the next generation—to the next level of glory—which is passed on to the next generation—to the next level of glory—which is passed on to the next generation—and so on, until there is a generation that cries out, *"The kingdom of the world has become the kingdom of our Lord and of His Christ, and He will reign for ever and ever."*[4] If the earth is going to be filled with the glory of the Lord like the waters cover the sea, as Habakkuk 2:14 says, then it's going to happen through a people who know how to pass the torch of God's Presence from one generation to the next.

What's This? Some New *Style* of Evangelism?

Just think: If our generation of Christians raises our children to carry and transfer the torch of God's Presence, it wouldn't take many generations before the earth would be filled with the glory of the Lord. You might ask, "What's this? Some new style of evangelism?" Of course not, but we have put knocking on doors ahead of dealing with our children's needs. This is why preachers have led evangelistic services while their children were in the alley shooting dope. Their passion for taking Christ to the world led them to pour themselves into reaching the lost even while their own children lived a life destined for hell.

Preachers are not the only Christians to fall into this trap. I have observed too many Christian parents who spend three or four evenings a week at church until very late at night, when they should be at home holding their children, playing with them, and reading them bedtime stories. While these Christian parents are in Bible studies, their children are at home watching seductive television shows.

It is a spiritual thing when we have fun and enjoy the children God gave to us! Sadly, far too few Christian parents value these times of playing with their children. It just isn't spiritual. But to the contrary, they often abdicate their responsibility and sell off their children to the world system so they can "do the work of God."

Instead of spending our time fighting the devil, we should spend more of our time nourishing and nurturing our children, which is a very real way of fighting the devil. As we take time to pour into our sons and daughters, the Kingdom of God is expanded because all that God is accomplishing in the hearts of our generation serves as a step, a platform, for our children's generation to move up higher in His purposes.

BY THE *Fourth* GENERATION

Many Christians thought that we were going to subdue the earth with radio waves or satellite dishes. I thought that we were going to subdue the earth with books. But do you know what we're really going to subdue the earth with? Our seed.

Think about it: If Christian parents pass on the torch of God's Presence to their children and prepare them to carry the torch to the next generation, it will be but a few generations before the Kingdom of God dominates the world. A few generations is not that long. It is to us, but in God's eyes it is barely a blink. It takes Him longer to yawn than it takes four generations to go by. The New Living Translation of Psalm 39:5 says, "...*An entire lifetime is just a moment to you; human existence is but a breath.*" One inhale and one exhale from God is how long our lifetime is to Him.

It is estimated that 25 million people in America gave their lives to Jesus in the early days of the 1970s charismatic movement. Imagine the impact on our country today if those 25 million people would have had a heart for the generations. Suppose those charismatics would have turned their children into the same kind of on-fire believers as themselves. The next generation of believers would have been 50 million strong. If those 50 million people had then carried the Word of the Lord to their children, as the Scriptures mandate, by the third generation there would have been 120 million radically committed believers; and by the fourth generation America would have been a nation dominated by believers.

It could still happen. If we train our children and impart our anointing to them, in four generations we could be the Christian nation our early fathers envisioned. If we never pass out another evangelistic tract, if we never have one more evangelistic meeting, but we just raise our kids the way the Bible tells us to do it, the glory of the Lord could indeed fill this country...and the world.

That's a pretty awesome thought. Consider how God has been pouring out renewal and revival on the Church during the past few years. This is not just to make us feel good; God is preoccupied with the generations.

WE HAVE A *Narrow* PERSPECTIVE

Unfortunately, the church system does not share God's pre-occupation. To the contrary, we have become such a selfish, self-centered organization that we are concerned only about our own needs. We stand in front of the spiritual mirror trying to make sure that we look exactly right, having no awareness of anything beyond ourselves. As a result, spiritual poverty has been perpetuated from generation to generation. We have developed a "just get me through this day" way of life that is the lifestyle of a survivor, not an overcomer.

Being an overcomer is not something you can work up in yourself. You cannot attain that lifestyle by confessing it or claiming it. The overcoming way of life was purchased for you on the Cross of Calvary. It is God's gift; an inner, God-birthed conviction that He has something better for you in this life than this world has to offer.

Thus, the goal of all Christian parents should be to pour the power, truth, and love of the living God into young people. Then, instead of kids who struggle all week with the lure of sin, we would have teenagers in hot pursuit of their Lord. Sinful behavior would be the last thing on their minds because all they would want to think about is Him! Our children would be consumed with wanting to possess all that the Lord has for them; to live the full, abundant life He has promised.

A *Symbolic* THREESOME

In the Old Testament there are many symbolic threesomes. One example is Egypt, the wilderness, and the Promised Land of Canaan. These three locations outline the journey of the children of Israel as Moses led them from Egypt, through the wilderness, and finally into the Promised Land. Symbolically,

Christians must choose which of these three conditions of life they will live in.

Egypt is symbolic of cultural Christianity. In this condition, people live with little consideration of their Christian experience. It is the place where adults and children grow up and journey on their own, being unattached and uncaring about most eternal things. For the most part they are unaware of God's dream for them. These are believers who live in the context of a free society where a person grows up and becomes whatever he wants to become.

From Egypt God brought His people into the wilderness, a place of deliverance. Christians who live in the symbolic wilderness live in spiritual self-gratification. They are concerned about what God can do for them today. Therefore they want God to give them whatever feels good for the moment and meets their need right now, with no real consideration for the dream He has dreamed for them or for their children. These people use God to ease their conscience, but they never have the longing of their soul satisfied.

The nation of Israel had a survivor's mentality when they lived in the wilderness. They wanted God to "just get them through the day." There was no accumulation of wealth, no security, and worst of all, no destiny. All that Israel had was what they could gather to survive each day. They were constantly at war within themselves. They could never really choose God's plan over life as it had been in the bondage of Egypt. So they lived in a spiritual "no-man's-land." They did not go forward and they did not go back. They were stuck in selfish unbelief.

Although God provided for all their needs, He never intended that the people of Israel would remain in the wilderness. There was a better place. There was a Promised Land they could apprehend by faith. God had prepared a place of fullness, rest, and the joy of the Lord. It was a place of destiny and fulfillment, a place where man and God would walk together in intimate fellowship and harmony.

Christians today are no different from those early Israelites. We too have created a "wilderness" theology. We live with the attitude that God has provided barely enough power to let us squeak through the day. This is quite evident in the many believers who have the mentality that they are to be the lowest and the last, the worst dressed and the least educated. These Christians walk through life "suffering for Jesus" while the kingdoms of this world prosper and get a greater stranglehold on believers. That is hardly the abundant life Jesus purchased for us on the Cross! He wants us to live in the Promised Land.

Each person chooses where he or she will live. Some choose Egypt; others choose the wilderness; and still others, being satisfied with neither Egypt nor the wilderness, choose the Promised Land. These brave souls do more than talk about the Promised Land; they live there. As a result, these believers are winners; they are prosperous. They also give birth to a generation of children who are born in Zion, in the Promised Land of Canaan, where there is a cooperation and a co-laboring with God. This generation is raised in the environment of God's Manifest Presence. They live with a sense of His reality wherever they are.

Because they are continually in God's presence, these children born in Zion are trained and softened by the Holy Spirit.[5] They will be the head and not the tail.[6] They will be leaders, not followers—those to whom the nations stream.[7] They are the children who are destined to rule.

Full-Time SERVICE

When a young person gives his or her life to Jesus, the first thing the church system wants to do is steer that child or youth toward "full-time service." Our common definition of serving the Lord full-time is to be a preacher, missionary, worship leader, etc. That definition must change. It is absurd. As a born-again Christian, I serve God full-time. I am a full-time bearer of the good news. I am a full-time burning torch. I am a candle that cannot be hidden and a city set on a hill.[8] My service to the Lord is born from my relationship with Christ, not because I draw a paycheck from a church.

Christian young people can go into the arts, politics, education, communications, or the legal profession. They can go into any field and carry with them the Presence of God. The issue is knowing and fulfilling their destiny; and fulfilling their destiny means to be found in the will of God, no matter what that may be. Destiny is many-faceted. God may very well lead us in such a way that we spend some years doing one thing, and other years doing something else.

I started out as an elementary school teacher and loved it. In the multifaceted plan of God for my life, I journeyed on to pastor a church, establish a publishing company, and write books. There are still things on my heart that I want to do one day. I would like to teach in a university, be involved in theater, and run for public office. These things may or may not be in God's plan for my life, but I am open to growing and to moving into whatever arenas the Lord has for me.

Christians must be careful not to get locked into one thing. God's dream for you and for your children will include many adventures. When you speak to your sons and daughters about their future, instill in them a broad vision. Asking children what they want to do when they grow up presents them with the thought of choosing one career and being limited to that. Teach them instead that God's dream for them is a big dream. Whatever the Lord gives them to do now, they must serve Him with all their heart! But they must keep an open heart, knowing that at some time He may move them in a different direction.

We must understand that *whatever* we are doing, we are serving God; and not only are we serving God, we are also serving the people of the earth. We are showing them the Presence and power of the Lord. Wherever I am, whatever I'm doing at the moment, I have total and complete fulfillment because I am doing what the Lord wants me to do.

That sense of total fulfillment will probably occur outside of what we traditionally refer to as "full-time ministry." How can I not be in full-time service? Are my sons not my full-time sons? Of course they are. They are always my sons and never cease to be my sons. Because of this fact, they reflect who I am. They carry my genes within them, as well as elements of my personality. They display who I am to everyone they meet.

With God as our Father, we display to the world who He is. We are always His full-time, 24-hours-a-day children. We are His ambassadors.[9]

An ambassador is always an ambassador. His job is not from 9 a.m. to 5 p.m. When he has a weekend off, he is still an ambassador. He is a continual representative of the nation, the kingdom, that sent him. As Christ's ambassadors, we are citizens of an eternal Kingdom, and we carry the essence of who Jesus is to the world.

More THAN CARRIERS

You are a citizen of Heaven, a member of royalty, a chosen person of strength, compassion, mercy, and power.[10] You are a living representation of Zion, the city of God. All the streams of joy that are in God flow forth from Zion.[11] Revelation 22:1

describes these waters as a pure river of the water of life. It is flowing and is as clear as crystal, proceeding from the throne of God. The throne of God is in Zion, and this river of the water of life is intended to flow out through *you, God's ambassador!*[12]

You have more than an anointing. *You are a river!* Your anointing is something that is living and vibrant and powerful. This living anointing resides in you, and when you pour your anointing into your children, it flows like a river, for it cannot be exhausted. Your children will pass this river of life on to the next generation, and they to the next.

Whoever you are, whatever you've experienced, and wherever you think you are in life, you have an anointing that God wants you to pass on. It is the living, vibrant essence of His power that He has deposited in you. And you have no right to take it to the grave! Such is the passion of Psalm 71:17-18:

> *Since my youth, O God, You have taught me, and to this day I declare Your marvelous deeds. Even when I am old and gray, do not forsake me, O God, till I declare Your power to the next generation, Your might to all who are to come.*

You must not be satisfied to keep your anointing to and for yourself. You must not be content to have your own personal needs met and to be uncaring about the things that will happen in the future. There are people all around you who need you. They need your anointing, and they need your strength. They need God's living, vibrant power that lives inside of you.

ENDNOTES

1. See Psalm 145:4.
2. See Colossians 2:9 NKJV.

3. See 2 Corinthians 3:18 NKJV.
4. Revelation 11:15b.
5. See Isaiah 54:13.
6. Deuteronomy 28:13.
7. See Isaiah 60:3.
8. See Matthew 5:14-16.
9. See 2 Corinthians 5:20.
10. See 1 Peter 2:9.
11. See Psalm 46:4.
12. See John 7:38.

---∞---

Father God, thank You for Your Presence
in my life and the anointing
that You have placed in me.
I want to make a difference in the world.
I want to be one of the passionate
men and women of faith and vision
who are establishing Your Kingdom
in the earth now, today.

Please show me what I can do to see
Your glory increase in the earth.
Open my eyes to the opportunities
You send to me each and every day,
and give me the wisdom and boldness
to take those opportunities.

I also ask that You will give me a heart
to take all that You have placed in me
and pour it into young people;
not just into my own children, but into every
child whom You place in my life.

Thank You for those people who passed
the torch of Your Presence to me.
Now use me to pass it on. In Jesus' name, amen.

---∞---

CHAPTER THREE

The Torch
of
His Presence

I have to admit that I have not always sought to pass on the torch of the Lord's presence to the next generation. I was like Hezekiah for a long time. (Do you remember his story from Chapter One?¹) When I was a new Christian, I definitely lacked a generational attitude. I would say, "Lord, please let me do Your will, but get me out of here before the rough stuff comes. I can't bear to see what my children are going to have to deal with. I don't want to watch them or my grandchildren suffer." I had no understanding that *I could make a difference* in how their future would look.

But today I am not ready to turn my children and grandchildren over to the whims of a godless world or to a carnal, self-serving church system. As followers of Jesus, we have authority that is ours by virtue of our heavenly citizenship. We carry divine power that can change this world! This is true because the earth is the Lord's and everything it contains,² and as His children, it also belongs to us. It is ours, and I'm not going to sit back and watch it be overrun with evil. I want to preserve and establish godly standards for my children and their children and their children's children. I want them to have the power to live for the Lord and to so spread His love that the entire world is infected.

The world will change when we raise a generation with the wisdom and power to speak to society in terms they can understand. God wants us to establish His Kingdom in every phase of politics, society, business, and culture—to fill the entire planet with His glory!

Our usefulness to the purposes of God is definitely not confined to being a worship leader, a preacher, or a deacon. Nor is it our responsibility only to pray. That's how we used to think: Someone else would actually do the work. Someone else would confront the evils of the world systems that resist the purposes and power of God. We thought that the Lord would somehow look after everything, not realizing that He wants to use us!

That attitude is changing. We are beginning to understand that the "someone else" needs to be "us." God is calling us not only to pray for the solution, but to be the solution. He wants to fill us so full of Himself that we become the answer to the needs we see around us. We are the ones who need to build morality and holiness into our children. We are the ones who must be filled with the Holy Ghost, led by God's Spirit, and empowered to stand against the evils of our day. We are the ones who must establish His Kingdom upon the earth.

The Church must focus on preparing the next generation to mightily affect the world for Christ. We must prayerfully and systematically mentor our children. Mentoring is our holy responsibility, and we will discuss it more thoroughly later on in this book. It is crucial that we prepare the young people to whom we will pass the torch. As we teach them to honor the Light they are carrying, it will shine brighter and mightier than when we took possession of it many years ago. Then, when Jesus comes to our children's generation, He will find faith burning in their hearts.

THE *Blessed* HOPE WILL *Always* BE BLESSED

I don't know any Christian who doesn't long to see Jesus. I don't know any Christian who isn't looking forward to sharing eternity with the Lord. Too often, however, this longing for the future causes us to miss God's purposes for the here and now.

The Blessed Hope does not begin with the taking away of the Church or our arrival in Heaven. The Blessed Hope begins the moment we find the Lord Jesus and give our heart to Him; and it unfolds as we continually look to Him and seek to become like Him. In other words, the Blessed Hope is planted in our hearts when we first take Jesus as Savior; and it grows to maturity as we enthrone Him each day as Lord.

God wants us to see Him in the midst of our daily lives. He wants us to experience Him in the routines of each passing week and month. The Blessed Hope is seeing Him at work in our circumstances and allowing Him to form our futures. It is watching the dreams He has dreamed for our children come to pass. Truly we are fearfully and wonderfully made not just within our mother's womb but also in the crucible of life as the Lord, through our daily experiences and those of our children, molds us into His image and likeness.

Yet this wealth of experience, vast as it is, cannot contain the whole of the Blessed Hope. It is not confined to this day-in, day-out process of reformation and restoration. Rather the Blessed Hope will be revealed in the Second Coming of our Lord Jesus Christ as having a dimension that is much larger than anything we had anticipated.

I long for and anticipate the return of Christ to this planet to meet a triumphant Church who has both made herself ready and is desperately in love with His appearing.[3] I, like the ten virgins in Matthew 25, have trimmed my lamp with oil and am anxiously awaiting His arrival.

Nonetheless, we have done our children a great disservice in our teachings concerning the Second Coming of the Lord. For hundreds of years it has been one of the most misunderstood doctrines in Christendom. Generation after generation of Christians have been so preoccupied with being taken up that they have completely ignored their mandate to prepare their children to carry the torch of God's Presence into the future. In essence they have said, "Why spend time praying for children, discipling them, or educating them if the trumpet is going to sound and we'll all be in Heaven in the next week or so?"

"Where Is the *Promise* of His Coming?"

For teenagers, this message of the soon return of Jesus Christ has brought a false sense of urgency. Teens can get consumed in the immediacy of almost anything that is exciting. When they hear that Jesus is coming back any minute, it makes them work harder in the church and it keeps them in services—but only for a while. It keeps them from sin—but only for a season. Soon they begin to feel as though we have hyped them up for an event that may not happen. Adults have used their youthful zeal only to keep them under control. Our children are the last people we want to exasperate but they turn out to be the *only* people who are exasperated.

We gave our children a promise of something that did not happen. The natural progression of their thought process is most uncomfortable for us to consider: "Hmm, they told us there was a Santa Claus and there wasn't one. They told us there was an Easter Bunny and there wasn't one. They told us

Jesus was coming soon, and He didn't. I wonder what else isn't true? I wonder if the Bible is even true?" Thus we inadvertently engender doubt and disappointment in our children by teaching them things we are not actually sure of ourselves.

On the other hand, some Christian parents don't teach their children at all—or do so in only a half-hearted way—because they experience an inner conflict between their belief that the Lord is coming back soon and their long-term responsibility of raising their children to live for God. They think to themselves, *Jesus is coming quickly. Should I spend my time pouring into kids who probably won't even grow up, or should I go out and try to save the world?* That inner confusion in mothers and fathers has often resulted in the inadequate training of children because it just doesn't seem worth the effort.

What, then, should Christian parents do? The answer is to be found in understanding three key biblical phrases that have influenced teachings concerning the Second Coming of our Lord Jesus Christ.

"Occupy UNTIL I COME..."

I know a lot of people who feel it's a lack of faith if you don't believe in Christ's imminent return. Some go so far as to say it is heresy. But whether the rapture is going to take place this week or next year isn't really the most important issue. The crucial point is what Jesus meant when He said, "Occupy till I come."[4] Translations other than the King James Version say to "do business"[5] or to "invest"[6] until He returns.

We should be teaching our children the value and the power of establishing the life of Christ upon the earth. Jesus said, "When I come back, will I find faith on earth?"[7] He was asking, "Will I find Christians whose only interest is filling up pews? Will I find Christians so concerned with the things of the Lord that they have neglected the Lord of the things? Or am I going to find real faith? Am I going to find people who understand what it means to 'occupy'?"

How then should we live? I am ready to hear the sound of the trumpet at any time. I live in constant repentance and preparation so that if He should come in my lifetime, I am ready to go. In the meantime I have a committed, calculated plan to live my life fulfilling God's purposes. I am occupied with planting and establishing His Kingdom in the earth, which includes pouring into my children what God has poured into me.

The most important goal we can instill into our children is not the immediacy of the return of Christ, but rather the joy and power of being conformed into His image and likeness while here on earth.[8]

"BEHOLD, I COME *Quickly*"

Jesus said several times in the Book of Revelation, *"Behold, I come quickly."*[9] Believers in general have interpreted "quickly" to mean that He is coming soon. Well, we have to remember that those verses were penned about 2,000 years ago—and Jesus hasn't come yet. The believers in that era didn't just sit around and wait. Perhaps the early Christians had a different interpretation of *"Behold, I come quickly"* than modern Christians have.

What if Jesus meant, "Behold, I come quickly to *you*."[10] What if He meant that He will be quick to answer our prayers,[11] quick to heal us,[12] quick to deliver us,[13] and quick to give us favor?[14] What if "quickly" actually means that He will come "suddenly" to us, His temple?[15] Our interpretation of

"Behold, I come quickly" has established a doctrine of immediacy that has totally nullified other Scriptures.

"THY *Kingdom* COME..."

For hundreds of years Christians have prayed *"Thy kingdom come. Thy will be done in earth, as it is in heaven,"*[16] believing that the Kingdom of God will come when Jesus returns. This is yet another interpretation of Scripture that allows us to relinquish our responsibility of raising our children with a long-term view.

Jesus wants His Kingdom to be established on the earth *before* His return. This is clearly seen in His conversations with the Pharisees. When the Pharisees asked Jesus when the Kingdom would come, He answered, *"The kingdom of God does not come with your careful observation, nor will people say, 'Here it is,' or 'There it is,' because the kingdom of God is within you."*[17]

The Kingdom of God is "righteousness, peace and joy in the Holy Spirit."[18] It is a state of the heart. The Kingdom of God is established in our own lifestyle of personal repentance, in our own pattern of allowing the Holy Spirit to prick our conscience and convict us of sin. This condition of the heart is the bedrock foundation of God's Kingdom, with Jesus as the chief cornerstone.[19] Everything we accomplish in life, and everything we are, is to be founded upon the Lord Jesus Christ, with brokenness and repentance being our way of life.

Prepare YOUR *Children* TO LIVE

In the process of raising our five sons, my wife, Cathy, and I have trained them, among other things, for the possibility of the worst of times. We want our children to know how to stand in faith when circumstances are difficult. When fear and anguish, anxiety and confusion, turmoil and uncertainty crowd in and scream from a hundred directions, we want our sons to have the ability to hear God's voice and to experience His peace in the midst of it all.

This does not mean that we raise our children in fear. Quite to the contrary. Our children are happy and full of life. We are teaching them to live in the joy of the Lord and to be ready for whatever may come their way. We are building, planting, and preparing them for whatever the future holds.

WHAT IF THE *Second* COMING ISN'T *Coming* LIKE I THOUGHT?

God is not confined to acting according to how I believe He acts. Although He never violates the Scriptures, He does violate *what I believe* about the Scriptures. The Lord doesn't limit Himself to do only what I will accept. Instead, He is constantly trying to stir my spirit, increase my faith, and transform my mind to enable me to believe things I never thought were possible. Our goal as His followers is to walk in a state of humility and softness, to admit that perhaps something we thought, or taught, about the Scriptures is inaccurate. What if we will *not* be alive when He returns for us? What if our children or our grandchildren are the ones who will actually see His return? Will they be prepared? It's up to us to teach them how to live in faith and humility no matter what circumstances or tests they may face.

When I was 19 (which seems like 163 years ago), two young men knocked on my college dormitory door and said, "Do you know that Jesus is coming soon? If you don't want to go to hell, you need to repent of your sin and accept Him as Lord and Savior right now!"

There I was, Don Nori, the "yet-to-be-regenerated soul," standing—no, leaning—in the doorway. I had hair hanging all over my shoulders. I was blowing dope and listening to acid rock in a room filled with black lights. Here stood two guys warning me about hell. I looked at them and said, "I want to tell you something: I'm already in hell. I don't need a Jesus to save me from a hell after I die. Listen, as soon as you find a Jesus who can save me from the hell I'm in right now, then you come back."

I closed the door, and I never saw them again. But that encounter had opened something in my heart. It stirred a search within me. *Can I really experience God's love now*, I wondered, *or do I have to wait until I'm dead?* I had been raised in a strong Catholic background so I knew that there was a hell. I was afraid to die without Christ, but I thought that the pain of what I was in couldn't be any worse than going to hell. To me it was the same thing. Whether I lived or died I was in hell; so what did it matter?

The two men at my door had also said, "Every single thing that the Bible says will happen before Jesus comes has been fulfilled. He could come when you go to bed tonight, or when you get up tomorrow; and if you're not ready, you'll be lost. Our pastor says that all we have is five years, maximum. Jesus could come sooner, but it's not going to be any longer than five years."

THE *Coming* OF THE LORD TO EACH *Generation*

So here we are, more than a quarter of a century later, and Jesus hasn't come. What those zealous young men did that night is what Christians have basically been doing for centuries: warning people and waiting. And without a clear understanding of the future, the attitude toward children has been, "Just get them saved and keep them saved. Keep them as far away from the carnal, worldly, sinful stuff as possible, because remember: Jesus is coming at any moment!"

We have been so concerned about the physical Second Coming of Christ that we have forgotten that God has a purpose for every person who is born; there is a coming of the Lord, as it were, to every generation. Throughout history God has visited each generation with fires of revival; and each generation has thought that surely the end of time was approaching. As a result, they have not imparted the fire to their children. Indeed, their obsession with the Second Coming actually robbed their children of their hope and their future! *Let us beware lest we too rob our children of all that is theirs in Christ Jesus.*

The work of the Holy Spirit within us will turn our hearts to Him and away from the things that have haunted us our entire lives. We do not have to spend the rest of our lives in the torment of the pain of our past. Additionally, we do not have to see our children be cursed with the same maladies that have chased us throughout these many years. The Second Coming or the sound of the trumpet is not the most immediate issue.

We may be the ones who hear the trumpet, and we may not. So what can we do to make sure that when the Lord does return, He will find faith on the earth and in us and our children? How can we pass on the torch of His Presence with bold assurance, confident that our children will value and hold high the flame? How will our children live as free men and women in Christ?

The next chapters of this book will help answer those questions....

ENDNOTES

1. See Chapter One, pages 19, 20.
2. See Psalm 24:1.
3. 2 Timothy 4:8 KJV.
4. See Luke 19:13 KJV.
5. See Luke 19:13 NASB, NKJV.
6. See Luke 19:13 NLT.

7. See Luke 18:8.
8. See Romans 8:29.
9. See Revelation 22:7,12,20 KJV.
10. See Matthew 18:20.
11. See Matthew 21:22.
12. See Acts 4:29-30.
13. See 2 Corinthians 1:9-10.
14. See 2 Corinthians 1:11.
15. See 1 Corinthians 3:16.
16. Matthew 6:10 KJV.
17. Luke 17:20b-21.
18. Romans 14:17b.
19. See Ephesians 2:20.

PART TWO

THE RIGHT
OF PASSAGE

*The right of passage
is the right of the things of God
to pass through
to the next generation.*

---∞---

In those days people will no longer say, "The fathers have eaten sour grapes, and the children's teeth are set on edge." Instead, everyone will die for his own sin; whoever eats sour grapes—his own teeth will be set on edge (Jeremiah 31:29-30).

---∞---

CHAPTER FOUR

Sour
Grapes

"I will *never* act like my mother! When I have children, I will not treat them like she treats me!" "My dad never had time for us. He never listened when we talked. When I have a family, they will know how important they are to me!"

Do any of these statements sound familiar? Many of us pray, worry, and fret over things we saw in the lives of our parents or our grandparents. We vow that those things will never happen to us, only to realize that the very characteristics we hated in our folks are very much alive and well in our own hearts.

As parents, things become even worse when we begin to see these despised traits emerge in our children. We become disturbed when our kids act like we do! Instead of being annoyed at them, we should be upset with ourselves for having allowed these character flaws in us to pass through to them. When we see these flaws mirrored in our children, we often pray, "God, deliver them. Lord, set them free!" And do you know what God's response is to that prayer? *"Their deliverance is locked up in your repentance."*

Recognizing Generational *Iniquity*

About the time I was studying this issue, my son Joel said, "Dad, I can't wait to grow up! I want to be just like you!" I said, "Uh, well, uh, thank you, Joel," and I went into the bedroom and prayed harder than I had prayed in a long time. Joel's words kept echoing in my mind, "Dad, I can't wait to be just like you," and I was thinking, *Okay, Son, but let's define this a little bit.* Why? There are parts of me that I definitely do not want passed on to my children.

We pass on to our children *who we are*. Spiritually, some Christians pass on the mediocrity of a religious system or the lukewarm "hanging on until the end" attitude of the average churchgoer. If, however, we are carrying high the torch of God's Presence, that is what we will impart to our sons and daughters.

When it comes to our ancestral history, we pass that history on to our children by the way we choose to live. We must embrace our family gifts and strengths and refuse to live out the negative things like fear, sorrow, and depression. Our children are going to have enough conflict in this life without our giving them our generational baggage to carry. When we notice things that we have struggled with throughout our lives emerging in our children, we must deal with those things.

Repent...TO THE LORD, AND TO *Your* CHILDREN!

God will show us the negative patterns in our lives that were given to us by previous generations. We then have a choice to make. Either we will pass that trait on to our children or we will intentionally choose to repent and cut off that negative trait, refusing to give it the right of passage. To make that choice we must understand that whenever we are fearful, have a pattern of angry outbursts, or model any other form of negative behavior, we are teaching our children how to react in similar situations. We are allowing ourselves to be the channels through which the things we do not want our children to have in their lives are being passed to them. Thus, to stop the passing on of these negative generational traits, we must take the time to repent before the Lord. We must also take our children aside and ask for their forgiveness as well. "I was wrong. What I just did was a *sin*. I'm sorry. I have asked Jesus to forgive me. I asked Him to forgive me for getting angry with you. Will you also forgive me?"

When I repent to my children, I don't tell them I made a mistake. I tell them I sinned. Christian humanism has replaced the word *sin* in many instances with the word *mistake*. Let's call sin "sin." A mistake is a human error. Sin is a choice.

Whenever we display traits that we despised in those who went before us, we must be quick to repent, both to the Lord and to our children. We must also repent when we demonstrate something that came out of our own sinful nature. Whether it came from our ancestors or from us, we need to repent of it; otherwise it can pass through us to our sons and daughters.

When I humble myself and ask for forgiveness from my children, it has a powerful effect on their lives. I am teaching them, first, that anger has no right in my life as their father, and second, that it has no right in their lives.

Remember that our example is what will have the greatest influence on our children. We continually teach them by what we do. Our example causes our children to respond to circumstances and situations the same way we do. I really wish it was just as easy as casting out a devil, but it isn't. I have to repent and change my behavior.

WHAT ARE *"Sour Grapes"*?

The fathers have eaten sour grapes, and the children's teeth are set on edge (Jeremiah 31:29b; see also Ezekiel 18:1-4).

What are sour grapes? They are the character qualities or the inclinations toward certain behaviors that are handed down in families through the generations. Some might call them generational sins or familiar spirits. Whatever they are, our children should not have to deal with them! We are in Christ, and as children of God, we want *His* heritage and *His* character traits to rule us, not our own sin nature or the sins of our fathers.[1]

All of us have a heart to move on in our journey with the Lord. When we are young, or are new Christians, it's easy to see those things of which we need to repent if we are to move on in the Lord. In truth, we are usually very aware of the "sour grapes" in our lives and therefore constantly seek the cleansing of the Lord so that we can enter into and experience His purposes more fully. But sometimes as we mature, we start to think, *I'm okay. I'm in pretty good shape.* That kind of complacent reasoning will hold us back. Change is a process that is a way of life, a good way of life.

Those of any age who are growing in Christ understand that the transforming process takes a lifetime. When we hear the Spirit of the Lord saying, "I want to take you on," we know that means He wants to cut something off so that we can fly higher. This is true no matter where we are in our relationship with God. He wants to change something in the natural so that we can continue to pursue Him in the Spirit.

We should never think that God's call to go on into a deeper experience with Him happens without sacrifice... without change. That change doesn't always mean more time spent in prayer and worship. Our progress into God's purpose also includes allowing Him to touch those places in our inner person that need to be healed, allowing Him to pour into our lives those things that are lacking.

Our lives are skewed by what went before us. Many of us have an awareness that something deep within our being is negatively affecting our progress in life. Perhaps there have been times when you have been really excited about something God put on your heart to do: a change of direction, a different job, or a move into new arenas. Then, just as you're ready to do it, something holds you back. Some obstacle blocks the way, some fear paralyzes you, or a change in your circumstances prevents you from doing what you know the Lord said to do.

Perhaps you have been catapulted forward and then knocked back so many times that you aren't even sure you want to go ahead again. I don't know about you, but I don't have time to spend another five or ten years being launched into destiny, only to be wrenched back because of something that continually hinders my progress. God's purposes aren't fulfilled by people who know His will. God's purposes are fulfilled by people who *do* His will. You know this, but something keeps holding you back, and you are tired of the battle.

God wants to set you free so that when He catapults you, there is no string to the past to pull you back! Truly, your future does not have to be manipulated or controlled by the negative thoughts, ideas, fears, or soul ties that have impeded you in the past. There is a destiny beyond the natural realm waiting for you...and for each one of God's children.

Learn to *Discern*

We are all sponges. We are constantly learning and accumulating information. As we grow older, we should become better at discerning which things we should absorb and which we should not. Young children, however, are sponges that just soak up whatever is around them. That's the way God made children. As they grow and are exposed to more influences, we need to teach our children to discern. We must also carefully watch who has influence in their lives. It is certain that our sons and daughters will soak up everything they can, especially from those people who are in positions of oversight in their lives, such as pastors, teachers, baby-sitters, daycare workers, and extended family. Our children will trust caregivers because we, as parents, placed those people in authority.

"ALL THEY *Know* HOW TO DO IS *Open* THEIR *Mouths*"

When my twin brother, Ron, and I were kids, we found a robin's nest that had fallen out of a tree. Two little robins were in the bottom of that nest, doing what baby birds do: Their eyes were shut and their mouths were open in complete trust. The only problem was, they were trusting two kids who didn't know what to feed baby robins.

In the security of their nest, high in a tree and far from curious seven-year-olds, these little birds were safe. They would be fed only what momma brought to them. Once the nest was in the grubby little hands of my brother and me, they were in big trouble.

When we went to the refrigerator to look for something to feed the robins, we found the remains of last night's delicious dinner. Surely these baby robins would enjoy meat loaf as much as we did! They didn't!

Within 20 minutes, they were dead. We ran into the house saying, "Mom, we fed baby birds and they died! They died eating your meat loaf!" She said, "Well, the meat loaf wasn't for them; it was for you." By that time we were in tears as we protested, "But, Mom, they had their mouths open!" Mom's answer was profound. She said, "That's because all they knew how to do was open their mouths."

You see, something unnatural had happened. God made robins to build their nests high up in trees so that only they can get to their babies, and not inquisitive little boys. Robins know what to feed their hatchlings to ensure that they receive proper nourishment. When those babies were bumped out of the tree, they fell into the hands of strange kids. We had the right intentions, but no knowledge; and the baby robins did not survive.

God planned that parents would know what to feed their children. He designed families so that parents would not only feed their sons and daughters food to make them physically healthy but would also pour into them spiritual nutrients and strength to prepare them for life. We are born with our mouths open and our eyes shut, so to speak, confident that what is put in will be healthy and wholesome. Young children have an innocence and complete trust that allows them to be fed by the one whom they trust. That innocence remains in them as long as parents and caregivers are trustworthy.

When children do not receive from their parents the necessary nutrients, they spend the rest of their lives hungering for what they never got. If our parents fed us things that did damage, we spend our lives with inner pain, longing to be healed.

Honor YOUR FATHER AND YOUR MOTHER

"Honor your father and mother"—which is the first commandment with a promise (Ephesians 6:2).

When I gave my life to Jesus, I didn't know how to honor my parents. It took God several years to get through my stubbornness and show me my lack of honor, especially toward my father. Thankfully, the Lord showed it to me; I repented, and Dad and I had a couple of great years before he died.

There are sour grapes in our own lives that we do not want our children to emulate. There are sour grapes within us that have no right to affect our children. They have no right of passage. These issues of life are intended to be dealt with by us so our children do not have to wrestle with the same things we have always had to wrestle with. Repentance puts an end to those issues that haunt us and haunt our seed.

Sometimes we try to hide the sour grapes from our children rather than repent of them. By living in a state of repentance, it becomes much easier to forgive our parents—or the person who raised us—who also struggled with sin. When we see the frailty of our humanity and our own failures, we extend mercy, not judgment.[2]

How do we honor our mother and father while knowing very well that there are things in their lives that cannot be honored? We honor our parents in the same way we want our children to honor us, even though we are struggling with our sinful nature. There are many good, valuable, and powerful things in our lives that need to pass into our children. We want those positive things to be seen, even in the midst of our humanity.

I have met many adults who want to be close to their parents but don't know how to keep themselves from the things that so negatively affected them as children. So they simply cut off contact with them. They sever all memory and relationship in an attempt to save themselves the intense negativity and often, temptation, that they feel.

We need a greater understanding of the purposes of God through the generations. If we throw out our heritage and reject our ancestors, we also reject the things that God wants to pass through to us. We need to honor our parents for the good things God put in them for us, and to forgive them for those negative things that should not be passed on to subsequent generations.

The *Need* for Mercy Helps *You* to Be *Merciful*

When we recognize our own frailty, we can be free. I have been judged because I am overweight, as though that is the only sin there is. I once said to someone, "If your secret sin was manifested in pounds, how much would you weigh?" Now, that by no means excuses me for having a weight problem, but it does give understanding that we all struggle with something that is difficult to overcome.

The fact that some sins are more outwardly evident does not make them any worse than the more hidden sins. For some people, keeping weight off is not a problem, but they are chronic gossipers or they have tempers that are totally out of control. The more we are painfully aware of our own sin and the constant humiliation of coming before the Father, repeatedly asking for His forgiveness, the more we become people of mercy. Because we know the depths of our own struggle, we no longer judge other people, but are quick to extend grace and compassion that we ourselves desperately need.

A person who lives in a continual state of judgment toward other people is someone who has never touched his own sin. He has never recognized the depth of his own sinfulness; he has never really called upon the Lord for mercy. Jesus said that He didn't come to heal well people; He came for the sick.[3] The ones who thought they were well could not receive His healing.

We are all sick. One sin is not greater than another. The person who has been on drugs is no worse than someone who cheats on his tax return. The sin that your father committed is not worse than your sin of hatred toward him. We all need mercy and forgiveness.

In those days they will not say again, "The fathers have eaten sour grapes, and the children's teeth are set on edge." But everyone will die for his own iniquity; each man who eats the sour grapes, his teeth will be set on edge (Jeremiah 31:29-30 NASB).

What a wonderful relief to look back on those who hurt us so much and forgive them. What a wonderful relief to be free of their detrimental influence in our lives. We can put a stop to the wrong responses and negative behavior right here and now. As Jeremiah 31 reminds us, the sour grapes that our ancestors have eaten will not set our children's teeth on edge. Our sons and daughters can be free to pursue God's destiny without the added encumbrance of our sins.

ENDNOTES

1. See 2 Corinthians 5:17.
2. See James 2:13.
3. See Matthew 9:12.

---⚭---

Father, we come to You in Jesus' name,
and we thank You for Your grace.
Holy Spirit, help us to forgive and
to love and honor our parents.

Lord, we ask You to bring to mind
those things that have hindered us;
those places of unforgiveness and harshness
and bitterness that we have held.

Lord Jesus, You don't want us to
carry them anymore. Father, You want us
to release our ancestors so that the
blessing of the generations can pass
through us to our children.

The strength of our heritage is locked
in our past. Lord, we don't want to be the plug.
We want our fountains to be unblocked.
We want the power of Your Holy Spirit,
the fresh flow of living water,
to move through us and into our families.
In Jesus' name, amen.

---⚭---

I know that nothing good lives in me, that is, in my sinful nature. For I have the desire to do what is good, but I cannot carry it out. **For what I do is not the good I want to do;** *no, the evil I do not want to do—this I keep on doing* (Romans 7:18-19).

CHAPTER FIVE

Sweet
&
Sour

Within each one of us there is spirit and flesh, good and bad, sweet and sour. From Abraham, who is known as the "father of our faith," came both Isaac and Ishmael. Both spiritual and natural came out of the same man. We can read Abraham's story in the book of Genesis:

> *After this, the word of the Lord came to Abram in a vision: "Do not be afraid, Abram. I am your shield, your very great reward." But Abram said, "O Sovereign Lord, what can You give me since I remain childless and the one who will inherit my estate is Eliezer of Damascus?" And Abram said, "You have given me no children; so a servant in my household will be my heir." Then the word of the Lord came to him: "This man will not be your heir, but a son coming from your own body will be your heir." He took him outside and said, "Look up at the heavens and count the stars—if indeed you can count them." Then He said to him, "So shall your offspring be." Abram believed the Lord, and He credited it to him as righteousness (Genesis 15:1-6).*

God made a promise to Abraham that from his seed would come a great nation. The promise from God to Abraham was that a son of his seed would be his heir. Abraham believed the Lord, but time passed and the promised son was not born.

> *Now Sarai, Abram's wife, had borne him no children. But she had an Egyptian maidservant named Hagar; so she said to Abram, "The Lord has kept me from having children. Go, sleep with my maidservant; perhaps I can build a family through her." Abram agreed to what Sarai said. So after Abram had been living in Canaan ten years, Sarai his wife took her Egyptian maidservant Hagar and gave her to her husband to be his wife. He slept with Hagar, and she conceived. When she knew she was pregnant, she began to despise her mistress* (Genesis 16:1-4).

God had given Abraham a promise, but neither he nor Sarah could wait for it. They went ahead and moved in the flesh, in the natural, to produce what God had promised. The result was the birth of Ishmael through Sarah's maid, Hagar. In Abraham's life, there was that which was born of spirit and that which was born of the flesh. The word of the Lord was born of the Spirit, but the word of Abraham was born of the flesh.

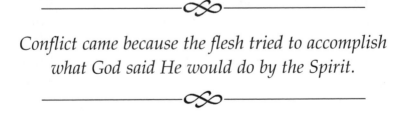

Conflict came because the flesh tried to accomplish what God said He would do by the Spirit.

Have you ever noticed that God never punished Abraham for Ishmael's birth? Our tendency is to condemn Abraham's actions, but even what he did in the flesh was done by faith. It didn't work because it was in the flesh, but it was still done in faith. Abraham believed God's promise, and he was going to make sure that it came to pass. He didn't understand how God was going to take care of it Himself. All Abraham knew was that he was going to be the father of many nations, and he reasoned, "If this is going to happen, I have to do something."

The birth of Ishmael added unnecessary heartache and suffering to Abraham and has continued to affect every generation since then with conflict. What Abraham did in the flesh was not according to God's plan and was not pleasing to the Lord. What pleased God, however, was Abraham's heart attitude of believing what the Lord had said. God never rebuked Abraham but referred to him as "Abraham, the believer."[1] This man's legacy is a legacy of faith, not a legacy of failure. Even having this failure in his life, he is remembered as our "father of faith" (Rom. 4:16).

> *Now the Lord was gracious to Sarah as He had said, and the Lord did for Sarah what He had promised. Sarah became pregnant and bore a son to Abraham in his old age, at the very time God had promised him. Abraham gave the name Isaac to the son Sarah bore him. When his son Isaac was eight days old, Abraham circumcised him, as God commanded him. Abraham was a hundred years old when his son Isaac was born to him. Sarah said, "God has brought me laughter, and everyone who hears about this will laugh with me." And she added, "Who would have said to Abraham that Sarah would nurse children? Yet I have borne him a son in his old age." The child grew and was weaned, and on the day Isaac was weaned Abraham held a great feast. But Sarah saw that the son whom Hagar the Egyptian had borne to Abraham was mocking...* (Genesis 21:1-9).

Ishmael mocked Isaac. The thing born of the spirit was living with the thing born of the flesh, and the result was conflict. The carnality of our minds is constantly trying to deride what is born of the spirit. Have you ever heard from God in the spirit, then allowed the flesh man in you to question what you heard?

> But Sarah saw that the son whom Hagar the Egyptian had borne to Abraham was mocking, and she said to Abraham, "Get rid of that slave woman and her son, for that slave woman's son will never share in the inheritance with my son Isaac." The matter distressed Abraham greatly because it concerned his son. But God said to him, "Do not be so distressed about the boy and your maidservant. Listen to whatever Sarah tells you, because it is through Isaac that your offspring will be reckoned" (Genesis 21:9-12).

Although tradition demanded that Ishmael be Abraham's heir, Ishmael was not the rightful heir. He was a man produced in the flesh—a flesh response to something God had said. In each of our lives, what is born of the flesh, like Ishmael, can live as an heir, live as the firstborn, until something of spirit comes along and displaces it.

You can have your whole life arranged, when all of a sudden, the spirit man invades the situation. Ishmael was the firstborn. He assumed that he was going to inherit an incredible amount of land and loot. The flesh man is always comfortable until what is born of the spirit arrives. As long as the flesh and the spirit are allowed to dwell together there will be a battle.

Is there conflict in your heart or your home? It is because the flesh and the spirit are in opposition with each other.[2] When we yield to the temptations of the flesh we sometimes allow the spirit man to recede. When we yield to the Spirit of the Lord, the spirit does not recede, but grows to become the dominant force. Then our inner man maintains strength and courage, and that which is flesh must go. The Bible promises that we will reap a harvest of what we sow, be it fleshly or spiritual.[3] This is why it is so important for us to become people of spirit. We must continually sow spiritual seeds and feed our inner spiritual man so that the spirit part of our being will be in control.

The Scripture says, *"Get rid of that slave woman and her son...."*[4] Cast out the flesh so that the spirit can take its rightful inheritance. Get rid of the flesh so that the spirit can have its rightful reward. As long as the flesh and the spirit dwell together, there will be no inheritance because there will be nothing but a life of conflict.

Abraham was given the tremendous promise that through him would come a people more numerous than the stars of heaven and the sands of the sea. The promise was going to happen through Abraham, but Abraham had two sides to him. He had the Isaac side, and he had the Ishmael side. The promise and the curse, the flesh and the spirit, were in the same man. Abraham tried hard to make the flesh man and the spirit man live together, but it never worked. What was born of God would live forever, but what was born of the flesh could have derailed the purposes of God.

Both Isaac and Ishmael live in us. We must repent of the Ishmael and embrace the Isaac part of our being. We must wrestle to the ground those sinful things that we struggle with, turning them over to Jesus, and repent of them so that our children don't have to fight the same battles. My children will have to fight their own inner war between flesh and spirit.[5] They will have enough of their own hassles to deal with. My children certainly don't need the turmoil caused by what I or past generations have dumped on them.

We need to conquer the "Ishmael demons" in our families to keep our kids from having to fight with them. I, personally, want to get rid of them all, here in my generation. I want my children to be free to spend their time establishing the

Kingdom, not battling the Ishmaels that I didn't have the courage or the heart to take care of in myself. When I raise the "bloody veil," the blood of Jesus, between myself and my children, the things in me with no right of passage are destroyed in my generation.

REGENERATION, *Not* DETERIORATION

The qualities and promises that belonged to Abraham flowed first into Isaac, then into Jacob, and now into us because we are his spiritual children.[6] We should go from generation to generation growing in strength. Second Corinthians 3:18 (KJV) says that we are being transformed from glory to glory, which means that the Kingdom of God is to be something that grows from strength to strength in us as the days go by. As each generation passes, the next one should be stronger. The Kingdom should be more powerful in our children than it was within us.

> *Therefore we do not lose heart. Even though our outward man is perishing, yet the inward man is being renewed day by day. For our light affliction, which is but for a moment, is working for us a far more exceeding and eternal weight of glory, while we do not look at the things which are seen, but at the things which are not seen. For the things which are seen are temporary, but the things which are not seen are eternal* (2 Corinthians 4:16-18 NKJV).

No matter what we try to do to prevent it, nature is deteriorating. I can take all the vitamins and food supplements I want, but I'm still deteriorating. The spirit man, however, grows stronger and stronger and from generation to generation. Nature tends toward destruction, but the Kingdom of God tends toward strength. When we plant the Kingdom of God in our families, our children will become stronger than we are.

A philosopher once said, "With the first breath you take as a babe, you're one breath closer to death." The whole world tends toward decay and ruin because of Adam's fall. If you leave anything out in the rain long enough, it will eventually fall apart, even if it takes 200 years. Buy a fresh bowl of fruit, and in a few days it is rotten. Paint a house, and it begins to deteriorate. Buy a car, and it wears out. Civilization also deteriorates. That is a hard fact for humanity to accept. In today's eroding society, deterioration is called "enlightenment." Deterioration of ethics and values is called "accepting alternate lifestyles."

Everything in the world tends toward ruin and decay, but a godly people or culture will be transformed from one degree of glory to the next. In Christ, we ascend, not deteriorate. We defy the laws of nature.

RELEASING THE *Power* OF THE *Generations*

When we use the term "passed down from our parents," we inadvertently accept the natural pattern of decline. We should be talking about passing things *on* to our children. As you look back at your family tree, you will see qualities that need to be passed on. All the people in your ancestral line, whether or not they served the Lord, were born with a destiny, a calling, and gifts from God.

Your ancestors had crafts and skills, abilities and talents, strength and courage that were given to them by the Lord. As you open your heart to them, everything that was good and wholesome and powerful in your family's heritage passes into you. It has the *right to pass*, and you become twice the person you otherwise might have been.

Within your children there is synergetic power because they get not only their own personal gifts from God but also all that you and your spouse pass to them. Out of your marriage union has come a life exponentially greater than your own. There's no end to the possibilities. God wants families to stay connected because that gathering together releases the power of the generations.

But we can receive blessings from others as well. Extended family, friends, members of your church, all have qualities that can be poured into your children as you open your heart to their love, friendship, and fellowship.

Do you know why the Body of Christ needs to be the Body? Because I need what your uncle has, and I need what your grandfather had; and you need what my great-granddaddy had. We begin to grow and are built together in Him. Then, as you give yourself to be mentored by a brother or sister in Christ, the power of the generations from that family comes to you, too.

When you look back at your parents, you will be able to find something you can be thankful for, something you can genuinely bless them for. Honoring your mother and father will open the door and allow you to receive the good qualities in their lives, qualities you were perhaps previously unable to see because of destructive circumstances. It is amazing how forgiveness clears hearts. The fog that clouded how we looked at our parents can be cleared away so we can see the good things—the gifts and abilities they had.

WE ARE *Imports*

Most of us are imports. Somewhere, one or more persons in your past had a driving passion for something better, so they took a risk. They left everything they had to come to a new land. Imagine, if you will, the fear and uncertainty with which our ancestors boarded ships and left their home countries.

My grandparents, both on my mother's side and on my father's side, were immigrants from Italy. They had such a longing for a better life for themselves that they sold everything they had and came across the ocean to a land where they couldn't even speak the language. Their dissatisfaction with what was and their hunger for something better was so intense that they came to America, the land of hopes and dreams.

I'll *Take* That!

When I think of the passion and the drive for something better that were in the hearts of my grandparents, I say, "I'll take that! I'll take those qualities as my inheritance!" Grandpa worked two jobs, 18 hours a day, to support seven children. I'll take that work ethic. I'll take that commitment to his wife and family. Those qualities have the right of passage. My mother's parents, the Pasquinis, had very creative business savvy. I'll take that! I'll take their tenacity and courage to explore the unknown.

Then I think about my father and his dissatisfaction with the fact that his creativity and potential were not being fulfilled. As a result, he started three successful businesses. I'll take his business and leadership sense. My father was a very loving, very tender man. I remember that tenderness. I'll take that. He was very committed to his children. I remember him playing ball with us after a 12-hour day. He was so tired that he could barely drag himself outside, but he did it. That's good. I'll take that into my life. It has the right of passage.

I look at the good qualities in both my mother's and my father's families and take them; and whatever good there is in me, I'll go ahead and give it all to my sons. Consequently, my family will not deteriorate from generation to generation; it will grow and be strengthened. The universe tends to deteriorate, but there is a never-ending growth cycle if Christ is the center of our families.

As Christians, we are new creations. Old things have passed away and everything has become new.[7] The promises to Abraham have the ultimate right of passage through the ages.[8] What is passed from Abraham to us? Faith and fruit-fulness. I will take Abraham's faith and fruitfulness! Obedience, a sense of adventure, and a willingness to lay everything aside and go where he had never been before— I'll take those qualities from Abraham as well. They, too, have the right of passage.

God gifted our parents and grandparents with the capacity to hear and respond to His voice. He gave them abilities to transform the kingdoms of this world into the kingdoms of our God. He has given those abilities to humankind throughout the ages. We need to begin to look back at where we came from and forgive those things in our ancestors that were the negative, sour side of their character. Because of our pain and anger, sometimes the whole parent is rejected. But when we reject the parent, we lose our heritage; we reject the blessing as well as the curse and end up losing the Isaac as well as the Ishmael.

Within your family lineage are inherent traits, talents, and gifts that need to pass into you so that your children can receive them. Do you want your children to experience the accumulated godly qualities passed to them from their ancestors? Do you want them to be free to pursue the purposes of God unhindered by the sour grapes you and your parents had to deal with? Then it's time that you choose to forsake both the sins of your ancestors and the sins of your own flesh. *Their deliverance is locked up in your repentance.*

ENDNOTES

1. Galatians 3:9 NASB.
2. See Romans 8:7-8.

3. See Galatians 6:8.
4. Genesis 21:10b.
5. See 1 Peter 2:11; Romans 7:15-25.
6. See Romans 4:16-18; Galatians 3:7-9.
7. See 2 Corinthians 5:17.
8. See Galatians 3:7; Romans 4:16.

---∞---

For the word of God is living and active. Sharper than any double-edged sword, it penetrates even to dividing soul and spirit, joints and marrow; it judges the thoughts and attitudes of the heart (Hebrews 4:12).

---∞---

CHAPTER SIX

No More
Sour Grapes!

Within your life there are opposing, powerful forces vying for preeminence: flesh and spirit, degeneration and regeneration, Ishmael and Isaac. Can you think of at least one thing in your life that you do not want passed on to your children; one thing that does *not* have the right to pass from you or your ancestors to the next generation? When you can admit and confess the Ishmael, the flesh man in you, then you can forgive the Ishmael in those who went before you.

Can you also think of some blessing from your forefathers and mothers that you want your children to inherit? Be sure to bless this Isaac part of your ancestors so that every good thing that God gave them comes to you, and thus to your children.

The blood of Jesus is that which separates the Ishmael nature within you from the Isaac. Then the Holy Spirit energizes the spiritual Isaac so that what is intended to flourish, flourishes and what is intended to prosper, prospers. Thus the strengths of your heritage are available to your children, and they are saved from having to fight the sins that beset their ancestors.

When this power of the New Covenant becomes active in our lives, we share in a building process that extends from generation to generation. Our children become stronger than we are now; and their children will be even stronger because we've learned how to repent of Ishmael and bless the Isaac within us.

God's intent is that our children will not fight the battles we fought. He wants our offspring to be free from those struggles so that they can concentrate on and put their energy into establishing the Kingdom of God in the earth. The Lord wants sons and daughters who will possess the Promised Land without having to fight the giants that we were never able to defeat.

THE BLOODY *Veil*

This whole concept of generational influence must be carefully taught and understood. Although there has been a great deal of teaching regarding generational curses, one crucial detail is not always made clear: When you become a Christian, you are a new creation, and the power of evil things from your ancestors is broken. You are no longer bound by their sins or their sickness. The enemy, who is a liar, doesn't want you to understand this. If he can get you to think that a curse is still on you, then it will affect you. In essence, you will invite generational curses by what you believe.

I rebuke and break off in Jesus' name any kind of attack, or any kind of remembrance of curses, that tries to touch my family. My prayer is, "The blood of Jesus stopped this curse when I became a believer. That curse cannot go through the bloody veil, which is the veil of His blood."

We all know of things in our parents' lives that we do not want repeated in our own lives. When you start acting like your mother acted, you had better stop blaming your mother, stop blaming the devil, and just get on your face and repent for your own actions! Remind yourself that any negative generational behavior has no right to influence your life. Its power was broken the moment you gave your heart to Jesus. The curse is gone. It did not get through the bloody veil of Calvary. If, however, you choose to act out negative behavior, you will create a whole new curse.

The *Right* of Passage *Through* the Bloody Veil

The blood of Jesus is a supernatural filter that allows what is righteous to pass, and what is unrighteous to be forgiven...not just laid aside, buried, or hidden, but forgiven. The only thing that has the right of passage through the generations is all that is born of God. The only thing that could go through Abraham's line to produce the promise was the seed of promise in Isaac. Ishmael did not contain the seed of promise, but the seed of flesh; therefore, his seed had no right of passage into the sons of promise.

There are things in me, Don Nori, that have the right of passage into my sons; and there are things in me that by God's grace are going to be filtered out by the bloody veil of Jesus.

Early in our marriage, in our limited understanding, Cathy and I determined that two specific things would not be allowed to be part of our home. The first thing that didn't have the right of passage was the typical Italian weight problem evident on my side of the family. Cathy and I resolved that our children were not going to be overweight. On Cathy's side of the family, there was a lack of expression of love. We determined that from the day they were born, our children would constantly receive affirmations of our affection and care.

As time has passed, we have noticed other character qualities and issues from our ancestors that needed to be cut off because they have no right of passage into our family. This has been an ongoing spiritual journey, and the Lord has been teaching us the power of the bloody veil along the way.

WINDOW *and* MIRROR

The blood of Jesus has the uncanny ability to be both a window and a mirror at the same time. Just as we are ready to pronounce judgment on somebody, somehow the window turns into a mirror, and we see ourselves. When I point my finger in judgment toward someone, the Lord shows me my own sin.

You might find that the finger you are about to shake at your father is shaking at you. Then your only recourse is to cry out to the Lord, "Have mercy! Lord, forgive him! Lord, forgive me!" And within that cry, you can discover a very, very powerful truth: *We learn to forgive the humanity in our fathers because the humanity is in us as well. Only then can we receive those qualities that have the right of passage.* If we reject the whole person—the entire father or the entire mother—we reject not only what we don't want, but the blessing as well.

DO I *Repent* OR DO I *Forgive*?

The whole issue actually comes down to our brokenness. When we really see ourselves for who we are, we find that we must be involved in two processes: We *forgive* for how we were *treated*; and we *repent* for how we *act*. We *forgive* our parents for the negative things, the sour grapes, that were in them; and we *repent* of the things we recognize in our own lives. These processes then create within us increased flow of the Life of God and genuine mercy toward others.

The right of passage is the right of the things of God to pass through to the next generation. The things without the right of passage, the sour grapes, we forgive, and they stop right there. It is important to understand that our forgiveness must not be from a condescending or arrogant attitude, thinking, *Those poor people just didn't know what they were doing.* We must not religiously forgive them from a position of superiority: *Well, I'll let them off the hook. They really blew it, but I'll let it go. If they were only as good as me, they wouldn't have had that problem.* This is not really forgiving; it is merely tolerating or granting amnesty.

Forgive *Your* Parents

When we look back and see the things our parents did that hurt us, we can choose to forgive them. Then all the strength and gifts that God gave them are free to flow into us. To take this a step further, we need to forgive our parents not just because we want their gifts, but because we know that unless we forgive them, we block up the fountains of life for ourselves, for our children, and for the generations to come. Without forgiveness, we are not just robbing ourselves; we are robbing our children of what their ancestors had for them.

All of us know that there are things in us that passed to us from our ancestors that we do not want. I mentioned in an earlier chapter the importance of asking our children to forgive us. How can we expect them to forgive us if we have not forgiven our parents? You may respond, "My parents never asked me to forgive them! If they ask me, then I'll consider it."

Your parents may never ask for your forgiveness. They may never apologize to you. They may not know that they need to! Nonetheless, I encourage you to find a place in your heart to forgive them. Do you want your children to harbor bitterness toward you for things for which you don't specifically ask for forgiveness? Jesus told us to seek forgiveness *as we forgive,*[1] that is, in exactly the same way we forgive those who sin against us. The Lord went on to say, *"For if you forgive men when they sin against you, your heavenly Father will also forgive you. But if you do not forgive men their sins, your Father will not forgive your sins."*[2]

It couldn't be much clearer. Do you want God to forgive you? Be quick to forgive other people.

WHAT CAN *You* ACCOMPLISH?

The seed that passed to you from your parents, grandparents, and great-grandparents contains every attribute you need to fulfill God's dream for your life. That seed contains the riches of your ancestry.

Truly, you are rich and you don't even know it, not understanding that within you is the wealth of the generations. You have abilities you haven't even begun to tap. Do you want to know what you can accomplish? Look back! In you is the power of every accomplishment and every positive and right thing ever done by your ancestors. Within you are the talents and possibilities that God bestowed upon your great-grandparents. Their gifts are in you.

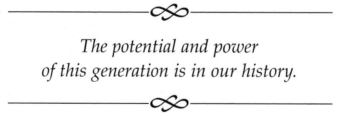

*The potential and power
of this generation is in our history.*

YOU *Hold* THE KEY

How do you release the riches and power of the generations in your life? You use the key: forgiveness. The place of forgiveness begins with an understanding of your own humanity; of where you have come from; of your own struggles and weaknesses. So seek to understand yourself. Allow your defenses and walls to come down. Don't be afraid to admit to the sour grapes in your life that you do not want passed on to your children. Repent of those things. They have no right of passage. Give them to your Lord and ask for His help so that those things will no longer rule you. When you are able to repent of your own sins, it becomes a way of life to forgive other people, especially your parents. As you forgive, the Lord will help you to appreciate them in a whole new way.

God will help you to honor your father and your mother. As you honor your parents, blessing them and forgiving them, you are accepting them; you are opening your life to receive from them; you are saying yes to God's gifts to you through them.

WHEN PARENTS *Don't* "DESERVE" *Honor*

In cases where you do not feel that your parents deserve honor or respect, there is a struggle. Instead of appreciation toward your parents, there can be very real feelings of hatred and disappointment. And yet, deep inside there is also a yearning to connect with them.

God planned for parents to pour into children. There is something within us that wants to be joined spirit to spirit so that we can grow. At the moment we come to a place of repentance from our anger and we can forgive our parents, the flow of God's life begins.

WHY, *God?* WHY?

God never intended for despair and heartache to be passed from parents to children. That was never His plan. The obvious question is, "Why did He let it happen?" Well, God didn't let it happen. What God did was give people a free will. We each have the choice to do either the right thing or the wrong thing.

Your parents had a choice;
now you have a choice.

You can choose, for instance, to continue to hate. You can choose to be angry for the rest of your life. If you choose that, however, you will never experience the peace of God. Nor will you know the power of God moving through the generations and into your heart.

So if the question in your heart is still, *Why did God let my parents do those things to me?* Remember that God didn't. They acted out of the free will He gave them.

God *Was* With You

You thought that you were by yourself those nights when you cried yourself to sleep, but you weren't alone. God was with you; He held you as you cried. You were just too hurt and in too much despair to feel His arms around you and to hear His loving voice. If you could have felt the presence of the Lord, you would have heard His comforting words; you would have felt His sweet embrace.

Perhaps you are still too wounded to feel the Lord's presence or to hear His voice. That's when you must simply trust Him; when, despite the pain in your heart, you must count on His love for you. Trust Him enough to repent of your hatred—perhaps even your hatred toward God Himself. Repent of your hatred toward your parents. No matter what they did to you, your animosity toward them is wrong. Ask God to help you with the forgiveness process. Ask Him to help you see your parents the way He sees them. Better yet, ask Him to help you see your parents the way you hope He sees you.

Seeing FROM GOD'S PERSPECTIVE

When I am angry with someone, the Lord often shows me that person the way He sees him. This softens my heart. When I look at people from God's perspective, I don't see strong, arrogant, callous people who just want to control or hurt. Instead, I see what causes them to act that way. Then I can't help but forgive them; I can't help but pray for them.

As you allow the Lord to show people to you as He sees them, the power of forgiveness begins to flow. Sometimes it's like a gush of the healing power of God. Then, as you forgive the evil, the pain is washed away and only the good remains and healing begins.

Forgiveness is the key that opens the dam, allowing the godly qualities that were in your parents, your grandparents, and your great-grandparents the right of passage. Forgiveness is the key that separates the negative, sour grapes in your life and allows the sweet and wholesome ones to prosper. Forgiveness is also the key that allows the river of life, which overflows with compassion, to flow through you to your children, your grandchildren, and your grandchildren's children.

YOUR CHOICE TO *Repent* AND TO *Forgive* WILL *Set* YOUR CHILDREN *Free*

A few years ago, Cathy and I were ministering to a bright and talented teenager. He was struggling to break the cycle of alcoholism and abuse. This young man had come face to face with some very dark things within his heart. He had confronted the "sour grapes" that had plagued his family for generations. We spent a lot of time with that young man over a period of several years. He worked at Destiny Image and lived in our home.

Cathy and I challenged our young friend to repent and turn his whole life, including his struggles, over to Jesus. His response to us was, "It's not worth it! This is too hard. I can't make it!" We asked him, "If you won't do this for yourself, will you do it for the children you may have someday? Will you let God have control of your life for the sake of your children and your grandchildren?"

By repenting of the negative patterns that were in him and had been so prevalent in the lives of his parents, that teenager was not only saving himself but was also rescuing several generations. By his response to God at that moment, he would end the abuse and alcoholism cycle. Sinful life patterns would be broken and cut off from affecting his descendants. Truly, the choices he made that day would have a tremendous impact on the future, giving the young man, his children, and his children's children the opportunity for a fresh start. In place of the dark things in his heart, God would light the flame of His Presence, which our young friend could then pass on to subsequent generations.

By allowing God to break the generational cycle in his life, that young man would be saving several generations. One day he would be able to tell his sons and daughters—and they in turn would tell their children—the great things God had done for their family. What our young friend would pass on to his future children would be only those things with the right of passage—those qualities that made it through the bloody veil: faith, stability, an awareness of God's love and mercy, and the torch of His Presence. Cathy and I challenged him to repent of his sin, to forgive his parents, and to turn to the Lord with all his heart.

Now I am presenting you with the same challenge. Perhaps, as you have been reading these pages, you have become aware of the need in your own life to repent of your own sinful behavior, to forgive someone for what he or she did to you, and to turn to God with all your heart. I urge you to do that.

I have written out some prayers to help you in this process. Please pray them right now, out loud, for your own sake, and for the sake of your children and their children and every child yet to be born into your family. The choice you make right now will affect their future. Pray them with faith, knowing that God hears you and will answer these prayers.

ENDNOTES

1. See Matthew 6:12.
2. Matthew 6:14-15.

*Father God, I thank You for Your mercy and Your love.
I believe that by the power of the Holy Spirit, and
through the blood of Jesus, You will set me free! Your
Word is sharper than a two-edged sword. It is able to
divide the soul and the spirit, the blessing and the
curse, the good and the evil that are in my heart.*

*Father, penetrate the hardness that sometimes prevents
me from responding to You. Lord, I ask for Your mercy.
I ask that as I go through life, others will forgive the curse
and embrace the blessing they see within me. Lord Jesus,
I thank You for Your strength that overcomes and defeats
every attack and every weakness in my life. Father, where
there are sins of which I need to repent, help me to repent.
Where I need to forgive, give me the grace and ability to
forgive. Where I need to ask forgiveness, help me to do
that too. Open the eyes of my understanding so that I can
see what has the right of passage and what does not.*

*Father, this day, I choose to repent. I repent of my own
sin.* (List sins that you are aware of: anger, hatred,
lying, procrastination, etc.) *As I consider my own
humanity, I repent for rejecting and pushing aside
those people who gave me breath. I understand that
within each one of us is both the blessing and the curse.
This day I look back on my parents and all those*

---∞---

who have gone before me, and I intentionally choose to forgive the curse and embrace the blessing. I cast out the sin nature of Ishmael and embrace the Isaac.

The sour grapes of my ancestors have no power to affect my life! I refuse the right of passage of anything that would want to kill, steal, or destroy me or my children. Forgive the curse, Lord; cover it and let Your blessing flow. In Jesus' mighty name, I declare that my children are free to live their lives and to serve God without being hindered from anything in our family!

Lord Jesus, may this word find its lodging in my heart. I pray that throughout the days to come You will continue to do Your work in me. Continually bring me to a place of repentance, healing, and wholeness. I thank You for Your blood that cleanses me, and for Your mercy that transforms me. You are a great and mighty God.

Thank You for calling me and wooing me to Yourself that I might accomplish Your purposes in the earth. Thank You for giving me the mandate to train up my children in the way they should go. Thank You, Lord, that You have given me the tools I need to pour into them, to equip the next generation to establish Your Kingdom here on earth. In Jesus' name, amen.

---∞---

PART THREE

PREPARING THE NEXT GENERATION

BY *Establishing* WITHIN THEM:
HISTORY, HOLINESS, AND *Hope*

In the previous chapters we learned to uproot the negative, detrimental elements in our homes and break the power of generational "sour grapes." The process of building the lives of our children, however, is much more than uprooting. It is planting, pouring in, and establishing what is good. Three good things that need to be securely rooted in our families are *history, holiness,* and *hope.*

Children need a *history* of what God did in the past that brought us to the place we are today. Then *holiness* needs to be established. Please note that I didn't say *legalism*; I said *holiness.* God wants the torch of His Presence to shine brightly through us, but that is greatly hindered if our lives are polluted. Finally, a groundwork of *hope* needs to be set in place.

Past history, present holiness, and future hope—when these three elements are planted in the lives of our sons and daughters, their hearts are prepared for God to reveal their destiny to them and shine His Presence through them.

*We have heard with our ears, O God; **our fathers have told us what You did** in their days, in days long ago. With Your hand You drove out the nations and planted our fathers; You crushed the peoples and made our fathers flourish. It was not by their sword that they won the land, nor did their arm bring them victory; it was Your right hand, Your arm, and the light of Your face, for You loved them. You are my King and my God, who decrees victories for Jacob. Through You we push back our enemies; through Your name we trample our foes. I do not trust in my bow, my sword does not bring me victory; but You give us victory over our enemies, You put our adversaries to shame* (Psalm 44:1-7).

CHAPTER SEVEN

Power
of
Your History

ISRAEL *Had* A HISTORY

Throughout Scripture, the Israelites told and retold the story of their deliverance from Egypt. Had God not rescued them from that place, they would have remained slaves. They were rebellious people, but in His mercy, God separated the Red Sea, led them through the wilderness, and brought them through the Jordan River into the Promised Land. It was not their own strength or wisdom but the power of God that overcame their enemies.

Israel was commanded to carefully pass her history on to each generation. As God's people rehearsed what He had done for them in the past, they and their children received an increased awareness of God's greatness and a deeper faith for the future. The psalmist declared that God's people would tell the next generation the praiseworthy deeds of the Lord so that *"...they would put their trust in God and would not forget His deeds but would keep His commands."*[1]

Personal HISTORY

This telling from one generation to another is just as important today as it was for Israel. Our children need to know what God has done for us.

Have you ever told your children your personal history? Have you ever talked to them about your life before Christ? Do they know of your struggles? Do they know your own stubbornness and unfaithfulness toward the Lord? It is certainly a humbling experience. I know, because I've done it. It's hard to tell your kids where you've been and what you've done. It's hard to tell them what dear old dad was like before Jesus came and changed him. It is hard to recount my struggle to follow Christ through the years. But do you know what that does for my children? It gives them a history. It gives them hope that following Jesus can most certainly be done!

If we are too full of pride or too embarrassed to establish a history with our sons and daughters, we rob them of a sense of appreciation of the life they experience now and the understanding that life can change, that it does change through Jesus' love. It is essential for them to realize that life would not be this way had God not come through and done great things for us.

What were the personal "Egypts" that God delivered you from? What desert experiences have you gone through? Israel's struggles in the wilderness were a result of their disobedience. You can't be afraid to tell your children of your own times of rebellion and disobedience. Yes, you love God, but that doesn't mean you never fall into sin. Without Him you are weak and frail; you have had to learn to depend on the Lord's strength, not on your own.

There was a season in the Nori family when God broke through time and space and, in His mercy, rescued us from our own land of Egypt. He broke into Cathy's life the day she almost committed suicide and into my life when I almost went off the deep end with drugs and alcohol. Truly God broke into the Nori family and established redemption. Had He not rescued us those many years ago, our situation and circumstances would be much different, indeed, than they are today.

Cathy and I have told our sons what we were like before we were Christians. I told them what I did in high school, when lying and cheating were a regular part of my life. While in college, I was involved with drugs, alcohol, and anything else you can connect with the hippie culture. Our sons know what they were saved from. They know that if God had not invaded our lives, they would be struggling with the same problems that Cathy and I had. Our children are well aware of God's faithfulness to us throughout the years.

A *Conversion* TESTIMONY

If you are a second, third, or fourth generation Christian, tell your children how you struggled as a child growing up in a Christian home. Tell them about the fears, anger, or anxieties that you had to repent of when you came to Christ. Tell your children how the Lord rescued you and gave you a new life. Your testimony does not have to consist of what is generally thought of as a conversion testimony. A conversion testimony simply describes how God convicted you of sin; it tells how He brought you to the point where you fell to your knees and repented. For some people this story tells how God saved them from drugs or alcohol. For others it is a tale of deliverance from hatred, anger, or cheating.

I began this book with the testimony of my friend from the People's Republic of China. When asked how he became a Christian, his response is, "Aah, five generations ago God broke into our family and established salvation with my great-great-great-grandfather. Hudson Taylor pulled him out of a ditch in Peking, took him into his mission, and nursed him back to health. My great-great-great-grandfather became China's first national Chinese preacher of the gospel. There have been five generations of preachers since then."

My friend goes on to say, "I am sorry to tell you that in my rebellion and my youthfulness I wasted the first 19 years of the salvation purchased for me. At the age of 19 I realized what I was wasting, and I repented. I gave my heart to God so that I could experience the salvation that the Lord began in my ancestors."

Don't cover up your past and try to paint a rosy picture of being some mighty man or woman of valor. Admit how you have struggled. Tell your children of your times of failure and how you called upon the Lord. Give testimony of how God gave you mercy and the strength to go on.

For my friend, salvation began in his family five generations ago. For some of you, salvation broke through with your grandparents or your parents. Or perhaps you are the first generation of Christians in your family. However long your family has served Jesus, be sure to preserve the stories of how God has intervened in your lives.

My sons know that their salvation didn't begin the day they personally received Jesus as their Savior. Their salvation actually began years ago when God apprehended Cathy and me. That is God's way. He breaks through time and space, introduces His covenant, and establishes His life in a family so that every generation to follow can live a life of godliness and fulfillment. His Presence, His love, and His life then increase with each passing generation of believers.

Family HISTORY

We've heard all the stories, and sometimes we laugh about them: "I worked for 50 cents a week at the Pennsylvania Railroad." Instead of laughing, we need to say, "Yeah, you did,

Grandpa, and thank God you did, or I wouldn't even be here!" I don't make fun of those stories anymore; I am grateful for them. Our children's grandparents are a valuable history lesson. Cathy and I teach our sons that those old stories show us the tenacity and hard work that is in our family. We can apply those qualities in our walk with God, enabling us to say yes to Him even when we don't feel like it.

Instruct your children to bless the generations that have gone before. Teach them that in honoring their grandparents they are saying yes to the gifts that God wants them to receive. Many of our forefathers came to this country without finances or possessions. What they did possess are the kinds of things we want our children to inherit. They came with courage. They came with a spirit of adventure. They came with a determination to achieve. There's hard work in those stalwart ancestors of yours!

Let me add a precautionary note here: Please use discernment as you tell your children stories of their grandparents and great-grandparents. Be careful that you do not impart any feelings of bitterness or frustration. *Do not* tell stories that might impart some of the negative family issues that have no right of passage. Consider how much, if any, of the negative information your children actually need to know.

When you are telling the "old, old stories," stick to ones that are exciting, uplifting accounts of faith and of God's provision. Even if your grandparents and great-grandparents didn't know the Lord as you do, the positive things in their lives were still gifts to them from God.

God has given gifts to every human being. As we yield our lives to Him, those gifts ignite into the full flame of fulfillment. If we live unaware of His love and unsurrendered to His Lordship, the gifts are still there, but they never become all that God wanted them to be.

When telling your children stories about their ancestors, watch for opportunities to draw attention to the God-given qualities in the lives of those people. Say things like, "Wow! What determination your great-great-grandpa had to take a wagon train to the West!" "Your great-grandmother quit working in the factory and started her own business. That took real courage in those days." "Your granddad was very musical. He played 11 instruments and was a one-man band!" Every quality in your ancestors is your rightful inheritance, and that of your children. Those things can pass through the bloody veil. Teach your sons and daughters to open their lives to the God-given qualities found in the previous generations, saying, "I'll take that!"

Faith HISTORY

Children love to hear stories of miraculous intervention. They enjoy listening to those stories over and over again because faith is built in their hearts regarding the reality of God. Take every opportunity to expose your children to the testimonies of Christian heroes. Read the wonderful stories of God's provision and care for His people throughout the generations.

I always loved listening to my father tell about God's supernatural care for him. One of my favorite stories was about the time he drove home from Pittsburgh to Hollidays-burg after a business trip. Just outside of Pittsburgh, Dad heard a loud "clang-clang-clang" under the hood of his car. He immediately drove at a lower speed and watched the gauges. Nothing seemed out of order, and there was no more clanging, so Dad reasoned that the noise must have been caused by something one of the tires had kicked up, and he resumed his speed.

About three hours later, just as my father pulled into the driveway of our home, he lost control of the steering. It was completely gone. He hit the brakes and turned off the ignition. When Dad lifted the hood of the car, he saw that the bolt that held the axle to the steering mechanism was gone. It was lying in our driveway. Upon closer inspection, Dad saw where that bolt had rubbed and rubbed during the previous hours of driving. My father realized that the clanging he had heard outside of Pittsburgh was the cotter pin flying out of the bolt. The bolt had stayed in place until it fell out in our driveway. What made it even more remarkable was that the bolt in that particular model of car was installed upside-down. *The cotter pin was on top*, not underneath. That upside-down bolt had stayed in place, holding the steering mechanism together, until Dad safely arrived home!

Every time we went on a trip, even before that particular incident, I can remember my father praying, "Dear Lord, send an angel to take hold of this bumper and get us where we're going." I pray the same thing before we go on any trips. I "took that" confidence in God's protection into my life. It is also a great story of faith for my children.

Don't Let Dad *Pray* for You!

I always lay hands on our sons when they are sick, especially when they have a fever. Almost immediately, the fever will be gone. One day, soon after our oldest son, Jonathan, turned 12, he came from the dentist's office with the bad news, "Dad, I need braces. Would you pray and ask God to fix my teeth?" I prayed. Every week or so I would lay my hands on his mouth and pray. Four years later, the braces came off and his teeth were fine. Around that time we were sitting at the dinner table and our third son, Matthew, told me his news, "Oh, by the way, Dad; I need braces." Jonathan immediately responded, "Don't get Dad to pray for you! Dad can handle fevers, but he doesn't do teeth. He prayed for me and I wore braces for four years!"

KEEP A *Memorial*

Hear, O Israel: The Lord is our God, the Lord alone. You shall love the Lord your God with all your heart, and with all your soul, and with all your might. Keep these words that I am commanding you today in your heart. Recite them to your children and talk about them when you are at home and when you are away, when you lie down and when you rise. Bind them as a sign on your hand, fix them as an emblem on your forehead, and write them on the doorposts of your house and on your gates (Deuteronomy 6:4-9 NRSV).

Of course, this Scripture doesn't mean that you take the Bible and tie it to your hands and across your forehead; it does mean that everything you do and everything you think is to be influenced and led by the Spirit of God. Your whole life needs to be based on the fact that Christ lives within you. Your thought life, the TV shows you watch, the articles you read, the jokes you tell—everything is automatically filtered through the bloody veil of Jesus. I want every aspect of my life to pass through that veil, and I want my children to develop that same pattern.

A memorial in Israel was like a plumb line. It was a foundation stone or a place where they staked out a portion of land. God's people could return to it not just to remember, but to know where they were. It was the place from which they could see both where they had come from and how far they still had to go.

The memorials we set in our children are the things they remember and always go back to. Recently I heard how an 83-year-old woman came to the Lord on her deathbed. This woman had not been a church-attender and had no recollection of any experience with Jesus throughout her lifetime. Yet, as she prayed the prayer of salvation, she heard the words of a song in her heart: *"My hope is built on nothing less than Jesus' blood and righteousness.*"[2] The woman wondered where those words had come from.

I know where those words came from. They were a memorial. Sometime, someplace, many years before, those words had been planted in her heart. As soon as she gave her life to the Lord, that memorial came back to her. It was her assurance that something had really happened.

OUR *Marriage* IS A MEMORIAL

Keep a memorial. With everything we do and every good thing that happens, we need to remind our children of God's goodness and mercy. My thoughts are always in thankful remembrance and appreciation of what God did when He saved us. He stopped the generational decline and brought our family to a place where we could begin to build the glory of God. Cathy and I often say to our sons, "If God hadn't saved us, we probably wouldn't be married anymore." Our marriage is a memorial, a reminder to our children of God's goodness.

The first day our oldest son, Jonathan, transferred from a private school to public school, he came home really depressed. When we asked him what was wrong, he said, "There are 31 kids in my class. Only three of us have both our original parents living at home." We were stunned by that statistic. Over the next few months, Jonathan's appreciation of our home life grew as he saw the pain and heartache that so many of his classmates were dealing with.

No matter how many psychologists and university studies might say that children recover from divorce, *they don't get over it.* Divorce is not a good thing. It's not something a child recovers from.

All five of our sons understand that they have God to thank for their family. They know that Cathy and I are human. They see us struggle with hurts and hassles just like other couples do, but they know that it's Christ who keeps us together. The Lord causes us to live a repentant life (most of the time) so that our marriage stays glued together. Our children have watched Cathy and I lean on our relationship with God to pull us through difficult times in our marriage. Their observations and the impact such times have had on them have been surprising. And, once again, we realize that our example is shaping the way they will deal with problems that arise someday in their own homes. They are learning to trust God in every aspect of life.

We must teach our children that they can trust God. Use every possible situation to give glory to the Lord for His protection and provision. Pray that the natural tendency in our children toward *self*-confidence is replaced with *God*-confidence! Build into their lives the foundational principle of faith in God.

ANCIENT *Foundation* HISTORY

Remove not the ancient landmark, which thy fathers have set (Proverbs 22:28 KJV).

"We must get back to our foundation! We must return to the foundation laid for us by our forefathers!" When you hear those kinds of vehement statements, you may wonder, "Well, what exactly is our foundation? Is it the traditional family unit? Are ethics, honesty, integrity, hard work, faithfulness, and compassion for the needs of other nations the foundation of our country?" The answer is, *"No, they are not."*

None of those things are the foundation; they are only the *fruit* of the foundation. The foundation established by our forefathers for this nation is that of a close, abiding, dynamic relationship with a living, vibrant Person, whose name is Jesus Christ. Once you have laid that foundation and there is a relationship—a connection spirit-to-Spirit with Him—the fruit of that relationship grows in your life automatically.

When we remove the Person of the Lord Jesus from the center of our lives and the center of God's purpose for humanity, we are open to every kind of subjective thought, and the end result is chaos. We are seeing this today in our country. Our society is degenerating because the foundation of God's Presence, the only true plumb line, has been removed.

Trying to restore values without first restoring God's Presence is like trying to hang fruit back onto a tree. I tried that once when I was a young boy. I picked about a peck of Bartlett pears from the tree in our backyard. They were as hard as billiard balls. When I proudly brought them into the house, I was quite surprised by my mother's response, "When your father sees those pears, you're going to be in big trouble!" Mom didn't tell me what to do; she just said that I was in big trouble. Being a resourceful young man, I found a stapler, glue, and scotch tape and got to work. I tried to put those pears back on the tree—but you know, not one of them stuck.

Changed values won't stick either as long as the plumb line of God's Presence is missing. We don't need to turn our nation back to values; we need to turn our nation back to God. Once Christ is restored to the nation, moral and ethical values will take care of themselves. These things are merely by-products of life that is filled with the Presence of the Lord. Abortion, homelessness, and drug abuse will be non-issues when Christ once again becomes our firm foundation, the Person on whom we base our existence.

In recent years there has been an attempt in our nation to re-establish the ancient foundation from the top down, beginning with the highest points of government. This will not work. Righteousness cannot be legislated. Righteousness is established first in the hearts of people; then it flows forth into every area of our culture. Our country will not be changed by wrestling our leaders to the floor and making them say "uncle"—or rather, "praise God." Our country will be changed when the *heart* of our nation is changed because repentance has taken place on a grassroots level. Righteousness cannot be legislated in a nation any more than it can be legislated in a church. It begins with real repentance from the heart.

The history we need to establish in the hearts of our children, the foundation upon which they must build their lives, is a relationship with the living Person, Jesus Christ. Our sons and daughters must serve a living God, a God who walks with His people and talks with them, a God who comes down to be with them.

Fathers, mothers, you must take the first step. Establish His Presence in your home. Demonstrate a living vibrant relationship with Jesus. From that ancient foundation will then come life and fruitfulness. Lift up the Man, Christ Jesus. Declare His marvelous greatness to your children. Teach your sons and daughters to put their trust in Him. He had a plan, and He has a plan. The Lord is faithful to a thousand generations.[3] He is the One who is our history!

ENDNOTES

1. Psalm 78:7.
2. Edward Mote. "My Hope Is Built on Nothing Less." Public Domain.
3. See Deuteronomy 7:9.

CHAPTER EIGHT

Power
of
Your Holiness

Most fatal car accidents occur either at dusk or at dawn—the time halfway between darkness and light when things are not clearly visible. The same is true in our spiritual lives. The worst place to be is halfway between darkness and light, the territory where you *think* you are all right but are unaware of the dangers that lurk in the half-darkness.

In this half-darkness, the conviction and leading of the Holy Spirit are shaded in your life. That's why the moment you take a step toward God—the moment you step into the light—sin often appears in your life.

This happens because you're getting into the light, where everything that was hidden in the darkness is now exposed. You see things that have been there all the time but were hidden by the darkness. Therefore, as you get closer to God's Presence and begin to see the sin in your life, you may think, "I'm backsliding!" Just the opposite is true. You are, in fact, in a very good place.

Explosive SITUATIONS

A child rummaging around a construction site might find a little box, which he happily plays with until someone tells him that it is filled with explosives. Immediately the child carefully sets down the box and runs! Why? His perspective has changed. The danger didn't suddenly increase—he had been in incredible danger the whole time. The difference is that the child is now aware of the danger because he knows what's inside the little box that he has been tossing into the air. In fact, when he is made aware of the danger, the danger actually decreases because he is no longer playing catch with the box.

So this is holiness: It is coming into an understanding of what is keeping you from your Lord. Holiness is a heart separation from the things of the flesh, by getting closer to Him. The closer we get to Him, the greater desire we have to flee the things of the flesh that will always distract us. Before you gain this awareness, you play with sinfully explosive things without realizing how dangerous they are. Only when you see the truth in the light of His Presence do you lay those things down, turn, and run from them.

Flee YOUTHFUL *Lusts* THAT WAGE WAR

Dear friends, I urge you, as aliens and strangers in the world, to abstain from sinful desires, which war against your soul (1 Peter 2:11).

There are some things that are obviously sinful: murder, adultery, witchcraft, drunkenness, etc. These sins are thought of as "the biggies," and most people know enough to keep away from them. The danger is in not being aware of the significance of the so-called "little things."

The acts of the sinful nature are obvious: sexual immorality, impurity and debauchery; idolatry and witchcraft; hatred, discord, jealousy, fits of rage, selfish ambition, dissensions, factions and envy; drunkenness, orgies, and the like. I warn you, as I did before, that those who live like this will not inherit the kingdom of God (Galatians 5:19-21).

Please notice that discord, jealousy, fits of rage, selfish ambition, and envy are listed there right alongside sexual immorality and witchcraft.[1] All the works of the flesh are dangerous and destructive because they keep us from God's Presence and His purposes for our lives. They pollute our hearts and cloud our ability to hear the Spirit of the Lord speaking to us.

Run from anything that stimulates youthful lust. Follow anything that makes you want to do right. Pursue faith and love and peace, and enjoy the companionship of those who call on the Lord with pure hearts (2 Timothy 2:22 NLT).

Run. Don't just walk, run! We must teach our children to run from sinful desires with the same intensity they would use to run from an angry bear. If they don't run, those sins will rule their lives. But by fleeing those things now, young people will develop a habit of resistance. Saying no to sinful things becomes a constant lifestyle of purity.

Let us remember what holiness is. It is a separation *to* the Lord. Separating ourselves to the Lord will give us desire and strength to stop playing with the temptations that will draw us away from Him.

When Paul told Timothy to "flee from youthful lusts,"[2] he was in no way limiting youthful lusts to "the biggies." All the desires of the flesh wage war. They bring conflict and do battle against the soul. Our soul includes the mind, intellect, and emotions. If the enemy can keep us preoccupied with temptation, fear, or guilt, then he can keep us from serving God. Scripture tells us to flee those things that are unholy, not just because they offend God, but because they wage war on the soul. Spending our time fighting to keep out of sin distracts us from what we are supposed to be doing for the Kingdom. The

Greek word for holiness is *hagnismos*. It literally means "a separation"—not only *from* something, but to something.

*Holiness is the process of separating ourselves to the Lord. In the process, it is discovering what in our lives keeps us from a close relationship with God, turning aside **from** those things, and of running to the Lord.*

When I was young, I used to play a game to see how close I could get my finger to the flame of a candle without getting burned. Well, that's pretty stupid, but sometimes we do the same thing with sin. We think we can get close to sin without getting burned, but if we persist in a sin, it will have damaging effects in our lives.

Many people wake up in the morning and find temptation lurking beside the bed. They say, "Lord, today I'm not going to give in to that temptation." All day long they fight it, until finally at night they drop into bed and say, "Thank You, Jesus, I fled youthful lusts today." Yes, they did flee youthful lusts, but they spent all day fighting instead of serving, so the temptation won the day.

The only time we fight the devil in our personal lives is when we are living too close to him! Because the war is over.

Run After God!

If you are running after God, the devil is nowhere near you. Therefore he cannot tempt you. So rather than having your mind so occupied with fleeing youthful lusts, repent! Don't spend the day with your finger as close to the flame as it can get without being burnt. Just keep away from evil things!

Nevertheless, you may still fall into sin at times, and even when you quickly repent, guilt may attack you. Why? Satan is waging war on your soul. He knows that you are forgiven, but he doesn't want you to walk in that forgiveness, so he sends guilt to assault your mind: *I failed; I blew it. How can I serve God the rest of the day, the rest of the week, or the rest of my life? How can I lead the Bible study? How can I even go to Bible study tonight, after what I did today? How can I be fit to raise my children? What right do I have to correct them when I'm doing sinful things?*

Sinful lusts do wage war on our souls, and when they disarm us, we feel like hypocrites. Then guilt torments our minds, sapping us of our strength, our courage, and our ability to confidently train our children in God's ways. This condemnation we battle is of the enemy. Stay away from sin and there is no war. Jesus took our sins, but He also took the guilt that comes with the sin.[3]

If you have been experiencing this internal warfare, repent! Turn to God and believe that He means it when He says, "You are forgiven. Your sins are removed as far as the east is from the west."[4] Get up and keep going! Run after God. Chase Him with such intensity that sin cannot come close enough to snare you.

External *Obedience* or Inner Life?

The Law is our tutor until grace comes.[5] Sometimes Christians have used the Law as an excuse because grace never comes. Grace is absent, however, because legalism never permits it to come—never brings us into God's Presence or gives us an understanding of a personal relationship with the Lord. A list of do's and don'ts can never bring us closer to God. All legalism does is give us a false sense of security about our future in Heaven. It does absolutely nothing to build the Kingdom of God while we are here on earth.

Following a list of rules is not what our children need. The easy way is to say, "Be holy or you're going to burn in hell. Be holy or you're going to get AIDS. Be holy or you're going to ruin your life." Holiness apart from a pursuit of God is like being all dressed up with no place to go. Yes, our children need to be motivated to be holy, but not out of conformity to a legalistic set of rules. *Motivation to holiness must come out of an awareness that the destiny God has planned will be achieved only in a life separated unto Him.*

Unless we establish this kind of aspiration for holiness (separation toward the Lord) in our children, they may grow up to be moral and to fit into a religious system, but they're not going to grow up to know God. In terms of the issues of the heart, those issues will still run rampant.

I remember a confrontation I had with my father when I was in high school. Dad said, "Don, you're going to get a haircut." I said, "No, I'm not." "Yes, you are!" "No, I'm not!" Finally, I went and got my hair cut, but I declared to my father, "My hair may be short on the outside, but it's still long on the inside." Although Dad could force me to conform to his standards, the rebellion of my heart remained.

That is what religious legalism does. It seeks to control the outward actions without dealing with the inner issues of the heart. If you are just trying to make your children conform to an outward set of rules and regulations, you're going to miss the point. They will have an external system of obedience with no true spiritual life vibrating within them.

*Holiness for holiness' sake is legalism.
Holiness that is pure, joyful, and exciting
is the result of relationship with God.*

Why does God want us to be holy? Is it because He doesn't want us to "smoke, drink, spit, chew, or run around with people who do"? No, there is a much greater purpose. God wants us to sanctify ourselves, to choose to set ourselves apart to be a people who will deliver the anointing to the next generation.

So give your children the ultimate reason for holiness: Live in the Presence of the Lord, where His dreams and purposes flourish. Show your children by example the rich benefits of pursuing and obeying God.

HOLINESS IS *Conquering* THE "ITES"

*When the Lord your God brings you into the land you are entering to possess and drives out before you many nations—the **Hittites, Girgashites, Amorites, Canaanites, Perizzites, Hivites and Jebusites,** seven nations larger and stronger than you—and when the Lord your God has delivered them over to you and you have defeated them, then you must destroy them totally. Make no treaty with them, and show them no mercy. Do not intermarry with them. Do not give your daughters to their sons or take their daughters for your sons, for they will turn your sons away from following Me to serve other gods, and the Lord's anger will burn against you and will quickly destroy you. This is what you are to do to them: Break down their altars, smash their sacred* *stones, cut down their Asherah poles and burn their idols in the fire* (Deuteronomy 7:1-5).

As the nation of Israel left the wilderness and entered the Promised Land, they encountered "ites" that they had not seen in the wilderness. Suddenly, every time they turned around they saw another one. The "ites" had full control of the Promised Land. They weren't even threatened until Israel crossed the Jordan River, which is symbolic of our humanity.

The same experience is true for us. The things in us that hinder us are in full control until we reach a point of surrender and commitment, saying, "I am going to possess my destiny! I want everything God has for me. The 'ites' must leave my land!"

God is calling His people to holiness. He is saying, "I am going to bring you into the land that I promised to you, but when I bring you into that land, the 'ites' are going to pop up. I will give you the power to destroy them. Don't make a covenant with them. Have no association with them."[6] Notice that the "ites" were not an issue until Israel moved across their humanity toward the Lord. It was only then that the "ites" would try to hinder them.

How does this apply to us today? There are "ites" in our lives that God wants us to conquer. If we are to conquer these "ites"—the idols that we have worshiped instead of God—we must stop making deals with sin. Don't say to your anger, "Stay back and be tamed; I'll only vent you when nobody's looking." Don't say to your poutiness, "You are not allowed to pout in public." And don't say to your addiction, "I'll let you out only in the privacy of my own home." Make no covenant with the "ites" that keep you from possessing all God has for you. Make no compromise with them.

Sin is choosing to go our own way instead of God's way. Every Christian faces this choice each day: Will I go my own way or God's way? Will I seek to know God and to live in His presence, or will I be so self-centered that I have little time or room for Him? The Christian life is a continual journey of making the choice to follow the Lord.

WHAT *Hinders* MY *Pursuit* OF HIM?

What prevents union with God is different for each person. Your idol may be reading newspapers: You have to read five newspapers every day. Thus, for you holiness means getting rid of the newspapers so that you have time to seek God. I, personally, don't read five newspapers a day; so reading a newspaper is not something I need to lay down.

Or perhaps television is your "ite." I once had a pastor who announced to the congregation that God had told him to get rid of his television. He preached that if we wanted to be holy, we needed to throw out our TVs. So incessantly did he badger the people about their TVs that I felt the need to ask, "Lord, do I need to get rid of our TV?" The Lord responded, "Do you know where the off button is?" "Yeah, I do," I answered. He said, "Then you don't need to get rid of it."

During that time period, I was functioning as a co-pastor in that congregation. One weekend, our church staff and leaders went away for a retreat. I helped my pastor carry his luggage into his hotel room. To my amazement, the first thing he did was turn on the television. The next morning I saw a fellow co-pastor, who was rooming with our senior pastor. This co-pastor looked awful. I said, "What's wrong? Are you sick?" He said, "I didn't get much sleep last night. Pastor watched TV until 3:30 this morning."

Throughout the retreat, I was in the lead pastor's room a number of times, and the TV was always on. Television was an "ite"; it was an idol in that pastor's life. God had told him to get rid of it for a very good reason!

After the retreat, I prayed again, "Lord, in light of this new information, I'm just checking with You again. Do we need to get rid of our TV?" God gave me the same response He had previously given, and now I understood what He meant, *"Do you know where the off button is?"*

What was an idol for that pastor was not a problem for me. What hindered his pursuit of God is different from what hinders me or another person. Some people have a lust problem so bad that they can't even have a department store catalog in the house. If a young lady has to spend two hours in front of the mirror every morning, she has an "ite" problem. It's not the makeup that's wrong; it is the two hours she spends idolizing herself.

I struggle with controlling my weight. Some people's struggles are hidden; mine is obvious. When I go out for dinner at an all-you-can-eat buffet, my family and friends may pile their plates high with rich foods and desserts, but I avoid those areas of the buffet. I know that all I have to do is breathe around that stuff and I put on pounds; so I try to stay close to the salad table. (It is obvious that I do not always succeed.)

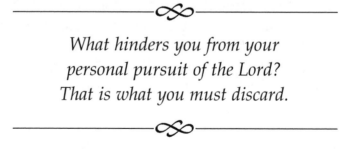

*What hinders you from your
personal pursuit of the Lord?
That is what you must discard.*

THE *Light* EXPOSES THE "ITES"

We have an expectation that everything will be wonderful when we leave the wilderness and enter the Promised Land. This is not true. Remember, the "ites" don't get stirred up until you get *into* the land of promise. It is His Presence that exposes them in our lives.

You may say, "Well, I'm not going to try living in His Presence, because every time I do, something goes wrong." That is exactly what needs to happen! The enemies of your soul hide until they are in the place where the light is so bright that they can't hide anymore. Stepping into the Promised Land, into the Most Holy Place, is your best hope of getting delivered from your inner enemies.

Religious people live in the shadows
where no one, not even themselves,
can see their true condition.

It's easy to sit in the seat of the scornful. It's easy to point and criticize. Religious Christians do this under the guise of prayer requests. They gossip and they slander those for whom they are to pray. Or they look at one another in judgment, trying to exalt themselves above everyone else.

If you are the kind of person who does this, start moving toward the Presence of God and see how quickly you become quiet! As you see the "ites" in your own life starting to pop up, you're so busy praying and repenting over yourself that you let everyone else alone!

Holiness Is a *Heart* Condition

Proverbs 16:32 in the New Living Translation says, "It is better to be patient than powerful; it is better to have self-control than to conquer a city." What a profound Scripture. It zeroes in on our own hearts, clearly revealing where the responsibility lies.

Who are you really, on the inside? What are the thoughts you permit to go through your mind? What do you allow your heart to ponder?

*Flee every sinful lust
that wants to wage war on your soul.
Run with all your might toward the Lord.
And you will be holy.*

ENDNOTES

1. Also see Colossians 3:5-9.
2. 2 Timothy 2:22 NASB.
3. See Hebrews 9:11-14; 10:19-22.
4. See Psalm 103:12.
5. See Galatians 3:23-26.
6. See Exodus 23:31-33.

CHAPTER NINE

Holiness
as a
Lifestyle

One evening our family was invited to join some other families who were getting together for fellowship. We discovered later that it was a token invitation; we weren't really welcome. When we arrived at the house, our sons, who are always excited to visit friends, were the first out of the car. Matthew reached the house ahead of his brothers, opened the screen door, and walked in. Then just as quickly as he had entered, Matthew rushed back out. It was almost as though he had been thrown backward. He hit the railing of the front porch and let the screen door slam shut.

I hurried to the front steps. "Matt! Are you all right? What happened?" I asked. Matthew, obviously shaken, said, "I'm not going in there first! Dad, you'd better go on ahead." I wondered what on earth he was talking about. I turned and headed toward the door. As I opened it, I was hit with what felt like a fierce wind. Tremendous spiritual resistance tried to block my way.

Immediately, I recognized that the enemy was trying to keep us from interaction with our friends inside. I cut a path through the resistance, allowing Cathy and our sons to enter after me. Later, I discovered that many who were there that night were being lured away from us by a wolf who had found its way into the sheepfold. We had unknowingly entered his lair, where divisive spirits ruled.

Matthew was a young teenager at the time. It is still a vivid memory for him, many years later. I thanked God that he had so keenly sensed the presence of the enemy. I was so thankful that he was tuned in spiritually and had discerned the spiritual opposition.

BECOMING *Spiritual* PEOPLE

Jesus asked the disciples, "Who do men say that I am?" The disciples answered, "Some say you're Elijah; some say you're one of the prophets coming back; and some say you're John the Baptist." Jesus said, "Who do you say that I am?" And Peter said, "You are the Christ, the Son of the living God." Jesus responded, "You are blessed, Simon Bar-jona!"[1] The word *blessed* means "fortunate and very happy." Why was Jesus so excited? It was because Peter was connected.

Peter had become a spiritual person. He had begun to discover that his motivation and life were no longer something that happened just in the natural realm. There was a whole new world out there, a whole new eternity of God in which Peter could participate.

Our children need to see, perceive, and live by the Spirit, not the natural man. As we plant in them a vibrant relationship with God, their conscience will become more and more tuned in and sensitive to the Spirit of the Lord, who is living within them to guide and teach them.

CHILDREN BECOME *Spiritual* PEOPLE
IN THE *Presence* OF THE LORD

Our sons grew up in the Presence of God. I have always prayed, "Lord, make our home a place where Your Presence is pleased to dwell." Of course, we know that He doesn't live in brick and mortar and curtains; He lives in us. That means if His Presence is pleased to dwell in our homes, it is because He is pleased to dwell in us. It is the condition of our spirit that saturates our home with God's Presence.

Playing Christian music or hanging inspirational pictures on the walls doesn't fill our homes with His Presence, although those things can be helpful. If we don't have a heart that is soft toward God, all the Scripture verses we stick on our refrigerators, and all the open Bibles in our living rooms, will not help us. Our homes are filled with the Presence of God because *we* are filled with the Presence of God.

Some of you are not in a position to control what comes into your house. I have some good news for you. Even in the situation where there is an unbelieving spouse, your home can be a place where God is pleased to dwell.

Your attitude of love and compassion toward your family is the real key. You are the person who creates such an atmosphere in your home that God likes to be there. If your home is *not* filled with God's Presence, the *last* person you should blame is your unbelieving spouse. The believer, whether it be the husband or the wife, is the one who has the ability to control the spiritual environment of the home.

An unbelieving spouse or child who does unholy things or watches unholy movies in your home will not diminish God's Presence. Those things will certainly affect their minds and hearts but they won't affect the spirit of your home because you are the gatekeeper.

A few years ago, we had a cleaning lady who watched soap operas in our house. We asked her not to do that, but she continued anyway. Despite the garbage that lady chose to fill her head with, those programs didn't affect the atmosphere of our home because she was not in a place of authority. I am the gatekeeper of my home. I'm the covering. Unless I, as the spiritual authority, open the gate to garbage, it cannot affect the spirit of our home. Any negative spirit that tries to come into our home must pass through me as the gatekeeper. If my gate is down, those things have legal entrance. For example, if I have sinned by getting angry at my children or my wife and there is not immediate repentance, I have opened the gate of our home to unholy, demonic influence.

COVERING YOUR FAMILY

This is how I pray for my family: "Lord, I cover my family and my home. I spread my spirit over my wife and my children, over our house and our animals, in Jesus' name." Just like a sheet over a bed, I spread my spirit over our family and our property to cover and protect them.

You may wonder why I include our animals in this prayer. A number of years ago we spearheaded the opening of a crisis pregnancy center in our community. As soon as the project began, we were under spiritual attack. Within one 24-hour period, our dog was killed by a car and our parakeet died. That little bird was literally singing one second and was dead the next! Then Cathy's favorite horse developed colic. Seeing that the horse was very close to death, we called the vet, then went out to the barn and laid our hands on that horse.

As we prayed, we discerned that we were battling a spirit of murder as a result of our confrontation against the murderous abortion spirit. I suddenly became aware that although I had covered my family, I had not included our animals in my prayers. I also recognized that had I not prayed for my family, that same spirit of murder might have touched one of our children. However, our animals were as close as those spirits could get to us. Ever since that time, I cover our property and animals, as well as our family, from the onslaught of the enemy.

It is my conscious choice to guard and protect my family. When I notice negative attitudes or actions in our children, I don't shrug them off by saying, "Oh well, kids will be kids." If I am properly covering the home and there is an atmosphere of the Presence of the Lord, peace will be clearly dominant in our home. If one of the children is troubled about something, I know that he has brought it into our home. So I take him aside and we talk about it. However, if I'm not covering my home, everyone could be troubled and I won't be able to discern the trouble because I am the one who has opened the doors of the spirit and allowed the enemy to get in. Then the enemy can run rampant through our home— spreading discord, unrest, and confusion. When I see those things in our home and recognize that I have been afraid, angry, or bitter, etc., I have to take responsibility for opening the door. I am the one who needs to repent. No one else is to blame. It takes my repentance to clear the spiritual atmosphere of my home.

There have been times when I have become so angry and upset about something that I thought to myself, *What you need to do is take a long drive.* I could never go farther than the driveway. I would sit in the car, but I wouldn't leave. I knew that for me to drive away was to leave my family uncovered; and I couldn't do it. If I voluntarily walked away in anger or any other negative attitude, I would leave the gate open and my family would be uncovered.

We must guard our heart attitudes. The Bible says that from our heart our mouth speaks.[2] Our words are very important. If you have an unbelieving spouse, don't complain or make accusations. Speak words of love. "Yes, I have an unbelieving husband, but I love him. I take care of him and I bless him." Don't make him feel guilty or preach Bible verses at him. Don't act in a religious manner, thinking that you have to show him the difference there is between you and him. Just love that spouse and let God's Presence flow through you in a very natural way. Often, an unbelieving spouse is more of a problem to the believing spouse than it is to the Lord. We need to trust the work of the Holy Spirit in our homes to do the will of God. If we can truly rest in that fact, we will be at peace. We will demonstrate love, patience, kindness, and every other fruit of the Spirit. This is truly the only way to win the family. Keep quiet and love them in every way we can.

CHILDREN IN *Church* SERVICES

Being in God's Presence has been a way of life for our family. Oftentimes at our meetings, the Presence of God would come with such force that we could barely worship. Sometimes a holy hush would sweep over the congregation. As we grew quiet, the children would also grow quiet, without our telling them to do so.

Some people might say, "The children grew quiet?! Why were they making any noise?" We have always kept our children with us in the sanctuary during the worship segment of the service, knowing that they cannot sit quietly. Young children and toddlers cannot be expected to sit still and be quiet for a prolonged period of time. But why would you want them to sit quietly!? Worship is an exciting and dynamic interaction with the Spirit of the living God. It's bound to get a little rowdy!

Early in our lives, we learned that a child's attention will come in and out during times of worship. When our children were little, Cathy brought a little carpet, which we spread on the floor in front of our seats. We allowed our sons to play with quiet toys and to look at books during worship. When the worship team played a song that moved their spirits, our children would jump up and enter in like they had been worshiping for hours. After the song, they would go back to playing. A bit later they would stand up and worship again. Then they would play, still enjoying the Presence of the Lord.

If your children stand beside you on Sunday mornings feeling angry and frustrated, uncomfortable and fidgety, they are getting absolutely nothing good out of being there. If your only concern is with making your sons and daughters look good to other people, you will teach your children to hate the fellowship of the spirit and the worship experience. It will be such a negative experience that they won't want to go. As soon as they are old enough to run away from church, they will.

As our sons grew up, their capacity to be part of corporate worship gradually increased. We helped them to make this transition into being a part of the entire worship experience. This process was different for each child. We would start by requiring them to worship for 10 minutes. That time frame grew to 20 minutes and then 30 minutes. I have so many memories of the ride home on Sunday mornings. I would say to Cathy, "Wasn't God's Presence amazing today?" And we would hear our children agree, "Yeah, I could really feel God close."

Our youngest son, Stephan, often ministers alongside us. When Stephan was ten years old, he had some powerful times praying for people at what we call "Regional Soaking Prayer Weekends." After one of the first meetings, Cathy was tucking him into bed well after midnight. Stephan hugged her and said, "You know what, Mom? Other than being born, today was the best day of my life."

You need to understand that Stephan has been to England, the Bahamas, Disney World, and all over the U.S. Stephan is a well-traveled child. He has experienced a lot of things, but "other than being born," that evening in the Presence of God was the best time he had ever had. Being used by the Lord to minister to people continues to be Stephan's favorite activity.

THE *Real* THING

I want my children to recognize and be accustomed to the Presence of God. I want them to love His Presence. It's where they feel safe, secure, and happy. Raising your children in an atmosphere of the Presence of God automatically puts them in a position to discern what's not acceptable, the vile and the profane. It's like FBI agents who become experts in distinguishing counterfeit bills by studying the real thing. When a counterfeit bill comes by, they immediately recognize it; not because they are familiar with the counterfeit, but because they are so used to the real thing.

Teach your children to enjoy the Presence of God. Expose them to His Presence so often that not only do they become accustomed to it, they also love the sense of His nearness more than anything else in this life. Then, when something vile or profane tries to touch them, they will immediately discern it. It won't matter what it looks like, how good it sounds, how profitable it seems, or how correct it appears, when something doesn't click they will stay away from it.

When our son Matthew was in high school, the young ladies were very attracted to him. One particular young lady was the most popular girl in the school; all the young men wanted to date her. Matt never asked her out on a date; and although she asked *him* out several times, he always said no. Matt told me how one of the guys at school asked him, "Hey, Matt, aren't you going to ask her out? Why not take her to a movie? She's gorgeous and she's crazy about you!" Matt's response was, "Yeah, she's gorgeous. She is beautiful—on the outside. But I can see what's inside, and I don't like what I see. I won't get involved with her."

When your children are used to the Presence of the Lord, they know when His Presence is absent. They know when there's something wrong, and what they should stay away from. No matter how beautiful that girl looked on the outside, Matt could discern that something about her would be big trouble for him.

The Inner *Witness*

I went on a lot of business trips throughout the years and there were occasional times when I canceled a trip because one of our sons felt uneasy about it. I remember our son Jonathan coming to us when he was a child. "Dad, I just don't feel right about this trip you are taking. Why do I feel upset inside?" I would say, "Do you know what that is? It is what we call a 'check in the spirit.' "

Even though sometimes I didn't feel that check, we had raised our sons in such a way that I trusted their discernment. We would talk about it and pray about it, and sometimes I changed my plans based on what they were picking up in their spirit. Was I submitting to my children? No. I was submitting to the witness of the Holy Spirit within them.

You have probably heard people say, "God told me not to...." They are really saying that they sensed an uneasiness in their spirit, a feeling that something was not right. Romans 8:16 says that our spirit witnesses with God's Spirit that we are His sons. We are in a constant state of our spirit touching His Spirit because we are in union with Him. By putting our children in an atmosphere where they consistently experience a close relationship with God, they will learn holiness. If something comes along that doesn't witness to that union, they feel an inner check. It is a caution that alerts them that something is wrong.

One night when our son Donald was about five years old, we were all watching a TV show called *The Dukes of Hazzard*. Boss Hogg, the villain of that program, had cheated someone out of $10,000. He held the suitcase full of money, raised his hands in the air, and said, "Praise the Lord! Praise the Lord! Praise the Lord!"

Donald sat right up, very indignant, slapped his hand on his knee, and declared, "He can't do that!" I said, "You're right, Donald. It was wrong for him to take that money." Donald said, "No, he can't praise the Lord for that! He did something bad!"

Throughout the years when we watched television and something came on that was questionable, Cathy and I usually didn't say anything. After the show was over, however, we would talk about it. That way we didn't cause frustration because we were preaching at our children while they were trying to watch the rest of the program. If the lesson happens 15 minutes after the initial event, it will still be effective. We may do more harm by interrupting something that they are intently interested in than if we just let it ride until the end of the show.

Our family has a few programs that we enjoy watching each week. Our married sons, Jonathan and Donald, will sometimes come up to us and say, "Man, wasn't that terrible. We couldn't watch the show last night." And I say, "Yeah, I shut it off too." Discernment has been wrought within them.

They know what to shut off, and they know what they can watch. Legalism controls outward behavior, but the Spirit writes God's laws on our heart.

Response TO THE INNER WITNESS

When young people are used to God's Presence, they will be able to immediately perceive the enemy. They will sense when there is a disruption in the spirit. They will feel an inner check. Teaching children discernment is teaching them to *respond* to the Holy Spirit when He gives them that check, when they sense a ripple in their inner peace. This will result in statements like: "I shouldn't be watching that. I'm going to shut it off." "I shouldn't go to that place." "I shouldn't have this person as a friend." "I shouldn't get in the car with that person."

Through daily exposure to television, radio, newspapers, and magazines, you teach your children to make decisions based on what they sense in their spirit. If you shield your sons and daughters from every outside influence, they will not learn discernment.

When our son Jonathan was a teenager, he was constantly changing radio stations while we were driving. I remember Cathy saying, "Jonathan, why do you keep switching channels? What are you looking for?" His answer was, "I don't want to listen to most of these songs. They stir stuff up in me that I don't want stirred up. But there are some songs that really have an anointing." It was interesting because the stations Jon was listening to were secular stations. There are secular songs that carry the voice of the Lord. There are songs that encourage, build up, and instruct. Our children love to listen to those songs.

I was raised in a private school under severe restrictions. The school only went as high as eighth grade, at which time everyone went into public school. A large number of those kids went totally wild when they entered the public school. Why? It was because they had been very sheltered and controlled, with no opportunity to make decisions. In that private school, young people were not taught to establish boundaries within their own hearts. They were just told what the boundaries were, and therefore could not discern the limitations for themselves.

Many high school kids who go off to college face the same thing. Because they've had limitations and restrictions so defined at home, they don't know how to make their own boundaries. They don't know how to define what is right and what is wrong because they never had the opportunity or the responsibility of making their own judgments. We cannot be everywhere with our children. If we take the time to expose them to the power of God's Presence and to teach them how to respond to the check in their spirit, we will save them (and ourselves) many heartaches.

HOLINESS IS A *Choice*

Holiness is a choice. Children must understand this decision-making process. They need to be aware that they are choosing between God and their own desires. Too many young people feel like they are choosing between their *parents* and what they themselves want to do. Or they are choosing between *religion* and their own desires.

As we bring our children into the Presence of God and they learn to love His Presence, even though there is a battle inside, they know in their heart of hearts what is right. Pray for your children and nurture the spiritual life within them. They will ultimately make the right decision to serve the Lord and not themselves.

The bottom line is not how well our sons and daughters are going to adhere to a list of rules, but how well they are going to hear the voice of the Lord. They need to be connected with the living God.

Our children must become spiritual people.

ENDNOTES

1. See Matthew 16:15-19.
2. See Matthew 12:34.

―――――――――――∞―――――――――――

*O my people, hear my teaching; listen to the words of my mouth. I will open my mouth in parables, I will utter hidden things, things from of old—what we have heard and known, what our fathers have told us. We will not hide them from their children; we will tell the next generation the praiseworthy deeds of the Lord, His power, and the wonders He has done. He decreed statutes for Jacob and established the law in Israel, which **He commanded our forefathers to teach their children, so the next generation would know them, even the children yet to be born, and they in turn would tell their children.** Then they would put their trust in God and would not forget His deeds but would keep His commands. They would not be like their forefathers—a stubborn and rebellious generation, whose hearts were not loyal to God, whose spirits were not faithful to Him* (Psalm 78:1-8).

―――――――――――∞―――――――――――

CHAPTER TEN

Embracing
Our Hope

The Bible is a diary of the family of God. It is a journal where family members can look back at the stories of their ancestors and see the Lord's faithfulness. God instructed Israel to give their children a *history*. He made them plant *holiness* in their sons and daughters because there was the *hope* of fulfillment beyond their wildest imagination.

Families today would be wise to chronicle the miraculous things God does for them and to pass that account from generation to generation. When we remember what God did, it gives us the hope that He will continue to bless our families, just as He did in the past.

God commanded Israel to keep a diary. Then He commanded that the generations to follow should *read* the diary. God wanted them to know, "Just as I was faithful to your great-great-great-granddaddy, I will be faithful to you. In the same way that I kept My word to Abraham and David, I will keep My word to you."

God HAS SOME *Promises* TO KEEP

God has some promises to keep. He is faithful to a thousand generations to those who love Him.[1] When God makes promises, He has one goal, one focus: That is to *keep* the promises He has made. Oftentimes we don't feel that we deserve God's promises. We might feel that we have abdicated our right to have what God wants to give to us. Actually we *don't* have any right to God's promises! He gives them to us because He loves us, because of the Cross of Christ. There is nothing we could ever do to earn God's favor.

If there is sin in your life that makes you feel that God's promises cannot be fulfilled to you, your responsibility is to get before the Lord, to repent from whatever it is you have done, and to turn the fulfillment of the promise back over to the Lord. When we are faithless, He continues to be faithful.[2] Even when we think that we are utter failures, God continues to strive with His people to bring us to a point where He can keep His promises.

God does not need to be begged, maneuvered, manipulated, or coerced into keeping His word. He makes promises because He wants to keep them. He is driven by His love for us. We don't have to go on a hunger strike to get God to keep His promises. We don't even have to remind Him to keep His word. It is the Father's good pleasure to give us the Kingdom.[3]

THE *Promise* IS BASED ON *Obedience*

Most parents have experienced something like the following scenario: "Hey, Dad, you promised that we would get a video tonight." To which you respond, "Yes, I did promise that we would get a video tonight. But in order to get a video you were supposed to clean up the family room and mow the grass."

"But I didn't have time...but...but...."

134

"Son, you didn't do what I asked you to do."

"But, Dad! You *promised* to get us a video. You're not going to break a promise, are you, Dad? You *promised* we were going to watch a movie tonight!"

That reminds me of how we Christians approach our heavenly Dad: crying and pleading with Him to give us something that He promised in His Word, and totally unable to hear the fact that the promise was based upon obedience.

WHICH *Road*: OURS OR HIS?

I had given a man directions to get from Philadelphia to our office in Shippensburg. I told him it would take two and a half hours on the turnpike. He was supposed to arrive at 9:00 A.M. When he finally rolled in at about 11:00 A.M., he was quite upset. "It's all your fault," he informed me. "You said that it would take two and a half hours! It took four and a half!" When I asked why it had taken so long, he answered, "I don't know. I followed the map and it took four and a half hours!"

This man had spread out his map, located Shippensburg and Philadelphia, and proceeded to choose his own route. As I listened to him, I learned that this man had taken secondary roads because he wanted to drive through Amish country. That cost him an extra two hours. I knew that I had nothing to apologize for. He hadn't taken the route I had specified. Had he done what I told him to do, he would have arrived in two and a half hours.

The more I thought about this, the more I realized that too often this is how we treat our relationship with God. God said, "If you will walk in My commandments, I will bless you. If you do what I tell you, all your needs will be met." He gives us a road to follow. Along that road are all the provisions for our journey: a gas station when we need it; a hotel when we need it; a restaurant when we need it. Everything will be there as we walk the road God intends for us to take. It is as though He says, "Go on this road. At each stage in the vision I have for your life, you will find what you need along the way. As you walk, you will see the book I want you to read or the person I want you to meet. Along this road will be the divine supplies for your journey."

Most of us, however, choose our own road. Then we get discouraged when the provision isn't there. The promise of divine supply is contingent on our walking the road God tells us to walk. He has not promised to provide for our needs when we walk a road of our own choosing.

IF WE *Obey*

Obedience is the criteria for receiving what God wants to give us. He is waiting, willing, and eager to fulfill His word *if* we will obey Him, *if* we do what He tells us to do and walk the path He wants us to walk. That is the stipulation for receiving the promise. You may say, "Well, then, it's not of grace, it's of works." To the contrary, God doesn't have to give us anything at all!

Who are we, mere human beings, to think that anything we do can be sufficient to earn God's grace and love? This is as absurd as an infant trying to earn his parents' love. Parents love their children because of who they are, not because of what they do.

The very fact that God *offers* to bless us is a result of His grace. As in the examples I discussed earlier, the result of staying on the designated path are all the blessings that are along that path. When we go our own way, those blessings are not along that highway. God is looking for people who will allow Him to bring them to a place of obedience and therefore alignment with His will so that He can fulfill the promises He has made. Hope is our response to our loving obedience to Him.

God's way is the only path of complete fulfillment in this life. If we truly believed that His plans for us are good, as Jeremiah 29:11 says, then disobedience would not be an issue. We would pursue obedience with all our heart.

His Highway is the highway of holiness, or separation unto Him, where all He has promised humanity awaits those who walk that way. When we separate ourselves to Him and His purposes, His promises naturally are fulfilled. His protection is assured and health is a way of life.

"THE LION *King*"

When Disney released this movie several years ago, little did we realize the prophetic nature of its storyline. "You are more than you have become" became a phrase repeated millions of times over the years. And for good reason. The longing of the human heart is for purpose. The longing within every person is to hear the words, "You have a reason to live. I have dreamed a dream for you, 'you are more than you have become.' " Nearly everyone who watched that movie would give anything to have someone of true spiritual caliber tell them, "You are more than you have become." Everyone wants to know that they were born with a purpose, that they have a reason to live. Talk about hope! Those words stir the heart with the realization that there is more in me than I have imagined and that there is hope for me to grow into someone I have up to now only dreamed about.

SOMEDAY, *When* I GROW UP

God placed eternity in our hearts.[4] There is a yearning within all human beings to have their life count for something bigger than themselves. God has planted purpose in us. As we grow, we have an increasing burden to know what that purpose is.

When you ask a child what he wants to do when he grows up, most of the time his response will be based on fantasy. A five-year-old boy may say, "I want to be a fireman." Then when he's seven he says, "I'm going to join the army and go to war." You know things are going to change, or at least you're *praying* things are going to change, because youngsters' decisions of what they want to do are rarely based on a sense of destiny; they are based on what's fun and exciting. Five-year-olds like to look at big fires and big red trucks with ladders and water splashing over everything. Seven-year-old boys like to imagine tanks rumbling through the woods and blowing up trees. They don't think about the fact that trees aren't the only things that get blown up when a cannon fires.

When we begin to mature, we must lay aside our childhood fantasies. God has planted something real in us. When reality begins to dawn in our hearts, and that can happen at a really young age, God's purpose and vision for our lives becomes more clear. True maturity requires that we truly become stewards of our purpose.

SOMETHING *Bigger*

Several years ago, I was going on a five-day ministry trip. None of my sons were able to accompany me, so I invited a friend of mine and his two teenage sons. The trip was a tremendous opportunity for them. They would meet some great men of God and be in meetings where the Presence of the Lord was very intense. But because it would mean missing a day of school, they were not permitted to go on the trip.

Sometimes we are "tunnel-visioned." We are so involved with the immediate and the natural that we don't see long-term benefits. Life experiences, especially on a spiritual level, far outweigh the importance of a day of school. My heart was grieved for those teenagers as I watched how the Lord touched young people in every meeting. I believe that they missed a divine opportunity to take some important steps closer to their destiny.

Parents, would you please pray for your children? Would you please begin to realize that there is destiny in your kids? Ask God what it is and begin to prepare them! Even if you don't know exactly what their purpose is, you can still give your sons and daughters love, security, and education. Give them a good home life. Model the kinds of character traits and qualities that will be needed no matter what direction life takes. *And, most importantly, take every possible opportunity to expose your children to the Presence of the Lord.* This kind of lifestyle prevents the curses of the past from visiting you and your children.

THE *Children* IN YOUR LIFE

Whether or not you are actually a parent, God has put children in your life who have a destiny. They are destined to rule and reign. They are destined to be leaders. Are you a little bit concerned about who will be our leaders in a few years? A recent statistic said that "between 26 and 30 million [American] adults aged 16 to 64 years were at the lowest level of basic [literacy] skills—roughly at or below a fifth grade level."[5]

As the world's systems decline, society has no hope. They have no alternative. Their best plans and their greatest thinkers have brought them to destruction and confusion. Their greatest philosophers have produced nothing for them.

On the other hand, neither has the current religious system produced what society needs. Clearly the religious structures of our day are as bankrupt as the world's systems. They will not, and indeed cannot, restore our society. It is the Presence of God, a living relationship with the living Lord, that will rescue our world.

OUR *Children* ARE OUR HOPE

God's dream for our children is their hope of a meaningful and fruitful life. If we will yield ourselves to Him and pass the torch of His Presence to our children, our sons and daughters will be the next generation of world leaders. We should be ready to produce a generation of believers who can rule the earth.

Does this sound ridiculous? It's not. All we have to do for this to happen is to change the world around us—not the whole world. We are responsible for our sphere of influence, to do what is at hand and to obey God in the position in which He has placed us. If we prepare our children by doing all that we should do for them, they will be the leaders of tomorrow. Our kids can truly rule the world. Few others are getting what our children get spiritually, emotionally, educationally, and culturally. With all we have for them, they can most definitely shape the future of our world.

Our children have a destiny. It is up to you and to me to understand this and to prepare our children to fulfill their destiny. I have no doubt that our children can cover the earth with God's mercy and love; this will mean that we, as parents, have taken the truth of the gospel and have imparted it to the next generation.

DON'T DASH THEIR *Hopes*

Throughout the years, Cathy and I have heard a multitude of plans from our five sons: "I want to take flying lessons." "I want to play professional football." "I want to start selling computers." "I want to start a paint ball business." As Cathy and I heard the ideas born in our sons' own hearts, we have encouraged and blessed them...and they prosper. Instead of trying to lay our expectations on them, we have tried to recognize what God has placed within them; then we have tried to draw that out, to nurture it, and to give opportunities for the expression of all that is within them.

No matter what ideas our children came up with, we didn't dash their hopes. Our initial response was never, "You've got to be kidding. You can't do that! We don't have the money for that kind of thing! People in our family don't become attorneys. Just forget about thinking that way!" When our son Matthew declared that he wanted to be a pilot, we didn't say, "You are not going to fly an airplane! The first time you go up, you'll crash and we'll never see you again!" We let him dream. As our sons' dreams ran their course, through their own experience they either embraced them or rejected them.

Years ago, Donald said that he was going to play football in college and then go two or three years with the pros. His goal was to save up enough money so our ministry, Mercy Place, could be free of financial worry. Never mind that only a small percentage of college football players, no matter how good they are, end up playing pro ball. We didn't try to discourage our son. Instead we said, "If that is the direction you want to go, we'll drive you to practices and do all we can to help you." Donald has long since discarded the idea. We didn't have to tell him that it wouldn't work; he found out for himself. He has since embraced the family business—no small destiny—and is being used mightily as he pursues his education.

Our oldest son, Jonathan, had some circumstances work out in such a way that he suddenly had $2400 in his bank account. Being a natural-born computer whiz kid, he got the idea of buying old laptops, fixing them up, and selling them at a profit. He said, "Dad, is it okay with God if I buy something cheap and sell it for more money as long as it's a good deal?" My reply was, "Hey, that's the American way. There's nothing wrong with that." Jonathan said, "I think I'm going into business!"

It was a creative idea born in our son's own heart because he had the freedom and liberty to explore, while still under our care. In the following weeks Jonathan asked a thousand questions, and Cathy and I guided him in his new venture. Our living room floor was often covered with computer components as he and his younger brothers, his "employees," worked to clean, build, and sell computers.

DREAM BIG *Dreams*

The family is a microcosm of what God intended the Church to look like. In our families we should allow our children to think and experiment. They are still attached to us, but as we nurture them, we must allow them to grow and to come up with new ideas, thoughts, and plans. Jesus is knocking on the door of each heart. He has something that is unique for each person to accomplish in the Kingdom. Consider the family that nurtures and grows and cares for one another; the family that hugs and heals and feeds; that lives and works together, yet permits each person to pursue and fulfill his or her own individuality and calling.

We should not be the ones who knock down our children's ideas. We should be right in there encouraging them, blessing them, and helping them. Whether they want to fly airplanes, play football, or be the president of the United States, let them dream. Let God adjust their dreams as they go along. Ephesians 3:20 says that our dreams are never too big. Let them dream and plan and try out the ideas they have!

"For I know the plans I have for you," declares the Lord, "plans to prosper you and not to harm you, plans to give you hope and a future" (Jeremiah 29:11).

God wants to keep His promises. Not only does He want to show us—and our children—the future He planned for us long before we were born, He also longs for us to fulfill every dream He has dreamed for us.

Our heavenly Father's dreams are different for each person. He has a specific destiny for each man and woman, boy and girl. That destiny can be fulfilled only by the individual for whom God planned it. When children know that God has dreamed a dream just for them, hope flourishes in their hearts. And when they know that their parents believe in them, there is nothing those children cannot accomplish!

Parents who fill their child's heart with hope, love, and the freedom to imagine, have few troubling spirits to deal with! Their children are so full of their future that they have little time for anything else.

GOD'S PURPOSES *Revealed* IN HIS PRESENCE

As our children spend time with God, His purpose for them will be revealed—for that is where God's purposes are discovered. So parents, watch carefully for every possible opportunity to expose your sons and daughters to the Presence of the Lord. Create an atmosphere of love, hope, and non-judgmental attitudes. God loves to dwell in an atmosphere like that! Your home can be a place where His Presence is pleased to dwell all the time. Do all in your power to provide an environment in which this can happen. Be diligent in giving God opportunity to unveil your child's destiny and to keep His promises. You will be delighted to see what your children, walking hand-in-hand with God, can accomplish.

OUR *Children* SHOULD EXCEED OUR *Accomplishments*

Children should always go farther than their parents. My father established three businesses in his lifetime. He was a hard-working man who focused on his family and their needs. As he taught us how to work with him, Dad would often tell us, "You will do better than I have done. I didn't learn this until I was 40 years old. You are learning these lessons at a much younger age!" I clearly remember my father saying, "I am doing all I can to help you. When I am old and gray, I will be proud to see how much more you have accomplished than I did."

Our children should not have to clear the same land and plow the same fields that we did. We need to plow and plant so they can reap a harvest from our labor and go on to bigger fields! We must broaden our vision of what the Kingdom of God is and of how our children can expand the Kingdom here on earth. I often say to my sons, "I didn't find the Lord until I was 20, and I didn't have my head screwed on right until later." (And some people still wonder about me.) "But now look at you; you were filled with the Holy Spirit and speaking in tongues when you were three and four years old! You are hearing God and responding to Him at such a young age. Just think how much more you are going to do for the Kingdom than I have done!"

What would our children accomplish if we would train them, point them toward the Lord Jesus, and tell them that God expects them to do better and to go farther than we have? With God's help, our sons and daughters will achieve much more than we could possibly hope, dream, or imagine.[6] Our children will take the torch and live with a greater sense of His Presence, a deeper awareness of His power.

ENDNOTES

1. See Deuteronomy 7:9.

2. See 2 Timothy 2:13.

3. See Luke 12:32 KJV.

4. See Ecclesiastes 3:11.

5. Patricia W. McNeil. "Statement on Adult Education and Literacy before House Subcommittee on Postsecondary Education, Training, and Life-Long learning" (Feb. 25, 1997). Accessed May 5, 1999, at http://www.ed.gov/Speeches/02-1997/98aetest.html.

6. See Ephesians 3:20.

CHAPTER ELEVEN

Be My
Hero

In a recent interview, I was asked, "Don, you have said that Pastor Ted Yohe mentored you. What did he do?"

"We played pool," I responded.

The interviewer stopped, pen poised in courteous unbelief. "You...played pool...?"

"Yep. We played pool. Ted had a pool table in the basement of the parsonage. We spent a lot of time there talking and becoming friends. It was over a game of pool that I learned to love him and his wife, Lou. We played pool and drank milkshakes." (Lou still makes the best milkshakes in four counties.)

I gave my heart to the Lord when I was in my sophomore year at Shippensburg (College) University. It was in that basement at that pool table that Ted Yohe, a Methodist pastor, carefully took me through the Scriptures, bringing me to the assurance of my salvation.

After that I met with Ted in a weekly Bible study. Eventually there were about 30 students who met every week with Ted. It was a really good time. Ted would do a short Bible study each week, and we tried to write down everything he ever said. Then we would tell him all the exciting things that were happening on campus, and we would pray together.

I remember one time, when I had been saved only a few days, I asked Ted, "Hey, if the Bible was written so long ago, how do we know that it still applies? How do we know that the Bible is still real today?" Ted calmly replied, "Well, what do you think?" And I said, "I don't know." With us that day were two other college students who had been Christians a few hours longer than I had. That made them the veterans, but they asked Ted the same question about the Bible's relevance. Ted's response was, "You fellows go ask the Lord what He says."

Ted was waiting for us the next week. "Well, what did the Lord tell you?" I said, "The Lord told me He doesn't change, and the Bible is the same today as it was then." The other two nodded and agreed: "That's what God told me, too." Ted just smiled. "You're hearing the voice of the Lord," he said; and that was the lesson.

One day Ted needed to pick up some out-of-town visitors at the Harrisburg airport. By that time I had been saved a few months. When Ted said, "Don, would you take my car and go to Harrisburg and pick up my guests?" I was shocked. Ted was well aware of my previous lifestyle. I said, "You're asking me to take your car and drive it one entire hour away to pick up your guests?" He said, "Yeah." I said, "Sure, I'll do it."

Ted and Lou's confidence in me was amazing...just amazing. But it was just what I needed. Their support was far deeper than a Sunday morning meeting. They cared what happened to me. They saw something in me that gave me the courage to look inside myself to find what they were so confident about!

To this day, I call Ted Yohe my pastor. Throughout the years he has remained a strong voice and influence in my life; and he has done so primarily by just loving me and believing in me. Ted has been a mentor, my mentor. To this day, his words to me are the most important words in my life.

THE "LAYING ON OF *Hearts*"

Mentoring is different than teaching. Teachers instruct you, but mentors love you. Because they love you, you want to learn everything they know; you want to become like them. Mentors cannot be assigned. You can try to assign them, but unless the mentor has it in his heart to really love the particular person to whom he has been assigned, teaching, not mentoring, will be the result. Mentoring is what Elijah did to Elisha. Elijah imparted *himself*, not just facts.

Some years ago I was ministering in Albuquerque when a man said to me, "Brother Don, I believe that you have something to give my son. I want you to lay hands on him. We believe in impartation. Every place we go we're going to have men of God lay their hands on our children, and we are going to lay our hands on them every day." My response was, "I'll tell you something, brother: You can lay your hands on your children all you want, but until you lay your heart on them as well as your hands, they will not receive the kind of benefit you want them to receive."

The ministry of "laying on of hands" in an impartation setting can mean a variety of things.[1] Through the laying on of hands we can impart healing, strength, encouragement, and spiritual gifts. People definitely get blessed and helped. But when you want a person's gifts to grow and develop to their full potential, that takes what I call "the laying on of hearts."

As we read the Scriptures, it is obvious that Paul was a mentor to Timothy. In First Timothy 4:14, Paul lovingly reminded Timothy not to neglect the spiritual gifts that had been given through the laying on of hands. The two books of Timothy are personal letters from a father, written to encourage and stir up the son whom he loved.

Love is the ingredient that causes heart growth. Mentors do not just lay hands on a person; they lay their hearts on as well. There is a difference between laying on hands to impart a blessing and truly loving someone into his destiny. Mentoring is saying to a person, "I'm going to give you what you need. I'm going to bless you and take care of you. I'm going to give you my time and my energy. I'm going to give you everything I have." We need to understand the commitment this entails. We need to count the cost.

Mentoring your children is not something you do for 45 minutes once a week. It is something you have to do every day of your life. It doesn't take minutes; it takes a lifetime. It is the kind of commitment that causes us to be joined in heart and spirit with our children so that we can pour our anointing into them, mixing with the River of God already within them.

STAYING *Connected*

How can we mentor our own children? How can we "lay our hearts on them"? In the busyness of our lives, how do we spend the time it takes? Let me tell you how it has worked for us. The main time that we have connected with our sons has been around the dinner table. Throughout the years, although both Cathy and I were involved in a growing publishing business as well as pastoring a fellowship of believers, our role as parents to five children remained our priority. I was home every night by six o'clock. The boys would try to have their homework and household chores completed by that time. We would sit down to dinner, and Cathy and I would start a conversation.

Our children would jump into the discussion and we never, let me repeat, we never shushed them. We were always interested in what our sons had to say, and we would try to pull out from them their ideas and feelings about whatever the topic happened to be. Throughout the conversation we would interject our ideas and standards and gently guide their thoughts. Night after night we would begin dinner at six o'clock. Many evenings we would still be sitting around the table at a quarter after eight, just talking and laughing and having a good time. If the younger children got bored, they would get some toys and come back and play at our feet.

The evening meal was the time we connected with our children, the time we looked at them eyeball to eyeball and gave them our full attention. You can imagine what dinner was like with five children around the table who all wanted to talk! Even as teens, our sons talked constantly. They told us about their day and about what was going on in their lives. Because of the lifelong pattern we have set, they know that we are genuinely interested in what they have to say; so they talk to us to this day. Our children have successes and joys, fears and failures, that they want to discuss. It is very important that parents keep an open connection with their children. For us, that connection was maintained every night around the dinner table.

In the autumn, when football season began and practices interfered with some evening meals, we started having breakfasts together. Thursday, Friday, and Saturday nights were usually dominated by football. So every Friday morning we got up early and went to a local restaurant for breakfast. We had so much fun that a few of our sons' friends from school started to join us. They wanted to connect with some adults who really cared about them. Often there would be almost a dozen people around the table at seven o'clock on Friday mornings.

MAKE *Work* AND OBEDIENCE *Fun*!

Except for football season, we ate together at home almost every night, and Cathy turned cleanup into a party. Clearing the table was fun! Before we got a dishwasher, I washed the dishes every night and the children gathered things up. I would stand at the sink, and everyone would bring the plates and serving dishes over while continuing the talking and laughing that had gone on at the table. It was work and play and family time all rolled into one. We had so much fun that I don't think our sons even realized until much later in their lives that it was work.

We used every household task as an opportunity to combine work, play, and family time. When there was work outside to do, we would do it together. When there was cleaning to do, we did it together. That way, the children received instruction, but they also learned to do it themselves. Because Cathy and I worked alongside them, our sons weren't overwhelmed by any task. Instead, they felt successful.

Assign children jobs they are capable of doing. For example, too many parents say, "Clean your room!" and then walk out and leave the kids to try and organize—without having been given some storage ideas or specific instructions. Messes can be very overwhelming. Think about it: Have you ever been told to clean up some big mess that you made in this life? Have you stood there in the midst of a monumental task, not knowing where to start? How would you feel if someone was there shouting, "You made the mess, now clean it up! I don't care if you don't know what to do. Just get busy and clean it up!" The challenge is to train our children, to teach them *how* to work without expecting them to do things they cannot do.

We tried to demonstrate both the joy of working and the joy of obedience. Through our own obedience to our heavenly Father, we tried to show our sons that it can be a joy for them to be obedient to us. We wanted our children to do their work with joyful hearts because it is a joy to obey; it is a joy to do what we are asked to do. Of course, we are human, and suffer with failure as often as the next person. But a quick decision to repent almost always salvaged the situation.

If your life with your children is both fun and instructive, they won't grow up being afraid to work or showing rebellion toward the authority figures in their lives. Your sons and daughters will be able to receive guidance and direction easily because their earliest memories of such things are happy. Their patterned response to authority is optimistic. They know that authority is there for their benefit, whether it be a teacher, a pastor, or an employer.

Submission is mandatory in our society. If we do not teach our children to submit themselves to authority, they will eventually learn it from someone else. If they continue to refuse to learn submission on their own, one day a police officer will teach them or the court system will force them to submit.

Pouring *Yourself* Into Your *Children*

Children respond to love. That is why mentoring works. That is why government-controlled daycare systems, schools, and boarding schools will not work. In the life of a child, instruction from a book is not the primary influence; it is the touching of heart to heart. Once you touch the hearts of your children, they will learn everything from every book you set in front of them. They learn because they love you and want to please you. Few children learn just because they are naturally curious. They want to learn so they can take the "A" home and show it to their parents or to that person in their life who is a hero to them. They want to learn because they love and trust the ones who gave them books to read and ideas to challenge them.

By opening your heart and loving the children in your life, you will break down their defenses of fear and rebellion. There are children all around you: your own children, nieces and nephews, boys and girls in your local church. You can make a difference in their lives. Once you have washed away their fear, rebellion, and pain with your love, you will find children responding to you. They will want to be near to you. They will be ones to whom you can pass the torch of God's Presence.

BE A *Hero* TO SOMEONE

Crawl out from under your paradigm for a moment and consider how we teach our children in typical Christian settings. Here's a radical idea: What if we didn't have Bible studies every week, or even Bible stories or practical lessons? What if, for instance, there were people in our congregations who were not inclined to teach in a classroom setting, but the children loved them? Once or twice a month we would ask those people to take a Sunday school class and do it *their* way. What if those people ushered the children right outside and played softball or took them for a soda?

Our sons' favorite memories of Sunday school are of a man in our congregation who would load the kids into his van and take them to the local ice cream shop for an hour. He would buy them ice cream and they would just sit around and talk. To this day, that man is a hero to my sons. Life took our families in different directions, but for years our children bought that man a Christmas present. They still trust him and love him dearly. He has been a hero, an anchor for them, for many years.

Another major hero figure in our children's lives has been my friend, Dennis. Throughout the years, his household has always been open to our sons. People like this are pillars and anchors; they become the road signs that help children get through life. They become heroes.

Heroes Put a *Face* on God
Sam Antenuchi Was My *Hero*

Godly heroes can keep kids on the straight and narrow path. Yes, children must learn to love God; and yes, they need to obey Him; but heroes put a face on God. Heroes bring the reality of a supernatural being to a level where a child can understand. A ten-year-old doesn't always think to himself, "God sees me. God knows what I'm doing. God is watching while I'm taking this candy." Sometimes the child can't bring God that close to him; so instead, the child may think, "I'd better not do this. I don't want 'so and so' to find out and be disappointed in me."

In my childhood, "so and so" was a man named Sam Antenuchi. I grew up in a church that did not have much interaction among the people, but every Sunday Sam would make a point of making contact with me. He would put a hand on my shoulder, smile, and say, "Hi." Every week Sam would ask about school or about how my summer was going. Then he would actually listen to my answer! He was genuinely interested in who I was and what was happening in my life. I was seven years old and Sam Antenuchi was my friend.

As I grew older and was faced with temptations, I thought of how disappointed Sam would be if he found out that I had done something wrong. More than once that thought kept me from doing things that I knew I shouldn't do. By the time I was 13, Sam Antenuchi became a Boy Scout leader, and I worked closely with him. I loved Sam, and he could teach me anything. I listened to his every word; I also made the other boys listen. Sam Antenuchi was my hero.

AUNT *Izzie*

Another hero in my life was Aunt Izzie. She was very attractive and fun-loving but had never married. Every Sunday afternoon of my childhood, my brother and I would walk up the hill to Aunt Izzie's house. At one o'clock we would jump in her car and go somewhere. She took us swimming or to the train yards in Altoona, where we would watch the trains go underneath the 7th Street bridge. Sometimes we would go explore the countryside. As Aunt Izzie drove her car, we would tell her to turn right or left; and for one hour, we would try to get her lost. Sunday after Sunday, we couldn't wait to see Aunt Izzie. We loved her. She just gave us her full, undivided attention.

On Saturday nights around six o'clock, my brother and I, and sometimes our dad, would go up to Aunt Izzie's. At nine o'clock we would walk home. My mom would say, "What do you do up there all that time?" "Aw, just talk and watch TV." When we got into high school, Aunt Izzie changed her schedule around so that she could drive us to school in the mornings. Aunt Izzie was our hero.

PRAY FOR *Godly* HEROES

In the church setting, we really don't have time for heroes. When we think of heroes, we look at sports figures or rock stars who often end up failing in one way or another. Our children sometimes have the wrong kind of heroes. It's because we really don't give them the opportunity to have heroes in their own churches, neighborhoods, and families. People need to pray for heroes for their kids. They need to seek out role models—real live people whom their children can observe, love, and spend time with.

Our sons had a few sports figures throughout the years whom they admired. I didn't mind that because our children knew where to draw the line. They would say things like, "That guy is awesome, but he's such a jerk! He wants seven million dollars a year. That is just ridiculous!" If a sports hero went on drugs, my sons would be disappointed in him and never want to emulate him. National heroes would come and go, but it didn't shake our sons because they had enough local heroes in their lives.

BE A *Hero* TO YOUR *Children*

Parents, you can be the greatest heroes your children have. But if you are anything like me, you often don't feel like much of a hero. You may feel that you don't have much to offer because you see your own struggles, mistakes, and failures. But if your children love you, you are already their hero. They already look at you with admiration and a longing to be like you. In their eyes, you are the greatest person who ever lived.

Throughout his life, your child may not always call you his hero, but when he looks back and remembers, he will realize who you were to him. My favorite Mark Twain story is how, when he was 18 years old, he couldn't believe how stupid his father was. When he turned 21, Mark Twain couldn't believe how much his dad had learned in just three years. Of course, the moral of the story is that Mark Twain's dad didn't change much in those three years. It was the son who had gone through enough grief and turmoil to understand that his father's wisdom was true wisdom. He had learned to appreciate what his father said.

Put your family's needs above your own desires and you will continue to be a hero to your children through their teenage years. Maintain an atmosphere of hope and love and consistency in your family. Whatever standard you set in your home, that is the standard. Whatever peace is in your home, it is there because you have established that level of peace. Eradicate fear and discontent from your family. Cover and protect them with your prayers. Be consistent. Be strong.

YOU CAN *Live* FOREVER

One day recently I was really lamenting to the Lord, "I'm getting older. God, I want so much to affect the world for You! I really wish I could live forever." It was one of those conversations with God that are more like a monologue. You don't expect an answer. But as soon as I prayed that, God spoke clearly to my heart, "You *can* live forever."

"Lord, I know that I'm going to live forever with You in Heaven," I said. He responded softly, "If you pour yourself into children, you will live forever. Everything you are, everything you've learned, will be carried on into the future through them." In that moment I understood what God was saying. Everything I am, everything that's worth keeping, can pass on to them through the Bloody Veil, and in that way, I will live forever.

The anointing you have—your gifts and abilities—can effect change throughout the generations if you give yourself to young people. Whether you are a parent, a teacher, or a scout leader—whatever position you have that puts you in contact with children—you have an opportunity to impact their lives. You have a choice. You can simply be their instructor, or you can be a mentor by opening your heart to them. Mentoring is not so much what you do or say as it is who you are. If you will choose to be a hero to a child, your life will continue to influence this world long after you have departed from it. *The torch you light in the heart of a child will keep on burning.*

ENDNOTE

1. See 1 Timothy 4:14.

For though you might have ten thousand instructors in Christ, yet you do not have many fathers....Therefore I urge you, imitate me....Imitate me, just as I also imitate Christ (1 Corinthians 4:15-16; 11:1 NKJV).

CHAPTER TWELVE

Imitate Me!

"Imitate me....
Imitate me just as I also
imitate Christ."

If someone were to say those words to us, the rebellious (religious) nature inside would likely rise up with, "Imitate you?!" and we would pull out our list of things we consider to be wrong with the one we should *imitate*. Unfortunately for our rebellious nature, imitate is exactly what we must do. For in imitating, we admit that we have much to learn, much to understand.

The apostle Paul wasn't saying to imitate him as though he had already attained perfection. Perfection wasn't the issue. Paul was saying, "Imitate my pattern of love and mercy. Imitate my lifestyle of repentance and forgiveness."

Imitate me.
When I fail, I repent.
Imitate me.
When people hurt me, I don't hold a grudge;
I forgive them.
Imitate me.
When people do evil toward me,
I do good to them.
I love them and pray for them.
Imitate me.
When I get angry, bitter, or frustrated,
I cannot let it rule me;
I must repent.
Imitate me.

The people we mentor are usually well aware of the weaknesses in our lives. Never try to cover those things up. The apostle Paul declared that he was the foremost of sinners,[1] but he still said, "Imitate me." Although Paul claimed to be the least of all the apostles, and not even worthy to be called an apostle,[2] he still said, "Imitate me." We are to imitate Paul's heart, his brokenness of spirit, and his desire to be a father to his children in the faith. Paul knew that the qualities and patterns of his life were because of Christ who lived within him. "Imitate me," Paul urged, "as I imitate Christ Jesus."

GENUINE *Fatherhood*

There is a reason for the intense attack against fatherhood today. If fatherhood can be destroyed, then the seed that will carry the torch of God's Presence from one generation to the next will also be destroyed. If there is no seed, there is no harvest. If there is no harvest, there is no generation to carry the purposes and love of God through time. Fatherhood is the foundation and fabric, the very essence of how God's Presence is carried through the generations.

The words "imitate me, let me be an example to you" are such a challenge to Western culture that many feel an inner resistance rising up at the very idea. Your thoughts may immediately turn toward men with highly visible ministries who have fallen into sin. Carnal people who do not know how to forgive use those examples to even further erode genuine fatherhood in the Church.

When someone says, "Follow my example," a disdain may fill your heart, but I challenge you to rise above it. If you cannot accept the necessity of submitting yourself to the process of being trained, your children will never follow you; and if they do, they will follow you with the same sense of resistance and rebellion that is in your own heart.

RESPECT IS EARNED, NOT ASSIGNED

---

*From now on we look upon no man
according to the flesh but according to the spirit.*[3]

When we are being trained, it is easy to pick out shortcomings in the person who has given himself to us. My pastor, Ted

Yohe, often frustrated me. No, he often made me angry. I had about 40 or 50 things I considered to be wrong in his life. When I felt angry, I would pull out my list of Ted's inadequacies.

Then one day I realized why I had such a long list to accuse him with. I was being convicted by the Holy Spirit because of the kind of example he was setting for me. His example meant that I would have to change. As I watched the way Ted treated people and how he handled difficult situations, I felt guilty for the kind of person I was.

Ted never asked me to follow him. He never demanded anything from me or told me to call him "pastor." As time went on, I became aware of the fact that I wanted to please him. I wanted Ted Yohe to be proud of me.

Respect cannot be assigned; it must be earned. Ted earned my respect because of his love. I came to the place where I understood that my anger toward him was only because his life showed me my own faults. I had to repent of my attitudes toward him, realizing that the root of my anger was in the fact that I was just upset with myself.

Not Many *Fathers*

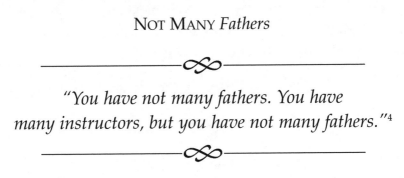

"You have not many fathers. You have many instructors, but you have not many fathers."[4]

You have a lot of people who will tell you what's right and what's wrong, but you have few fathers who will lovingly and selflessly commit to the placement of godly principles into your life. Many people are willing to advise you, but few will accept the responsibility of being a godly example to you.

Matthew 28:19 tells us to make disciples. This is a mandate for every believer. Some of you have been in settings where people in leadership positions have abused the discipleship concept. They put laws and restrictions on people to try to keep their churches full. Some denominations use membership as a means to strike fear into the hearts of the people. Members of the congregation won't leave for fear of losing their salvation, anointing, or ministry. That kind of controlling spirit won't grow a fellowship. It grieves the Lord. If the Holy Spirit can't keep someone in a particular fellowship, then laws and fear tactics aren't going to make that person a willing, contributing member of the body, even if you are able to bully them into staying.

We must not allow the fears and legalistic tactics of carnal men to keep us from the truth of the Scriptures. We can't let those people cause us to miss out on the beauty of allowing others to pour their hearts into us and, in turn, of our pouring our hearts into others. If you have been abused by legalistic men, choose to forgive those people who hurt you. Repent of any anger or bitterness you have carried, and ask God to lead you into healthy relationships where you can grow.

First, We *Need* Help

Being discipled often means to be trained in areas we don't want to be trained in and taught things we don't want to be taught. In essence, it means doing things that we don't want to do. Nevertheless, the choice is ours, not another person's. We decide if we will remain a child or grow up.

The world is full of children over the age of 40.

It's time to closely examine the path we have chosen for ourselves and to quickly turn to go God's way instead of our own.[5] The person who has learned in his heart how to yield to the Holy Spirit and has given himself to be built and strengthened in the purposes of God is the person who will accomplish his destiny. The rest will spend a lifetime talking about it.

Elijah TO ELISHA; *Eyeball* TO EYEBALL

Many people today never had the opportunity in their younger years to be trained in the ways of the Lord. In God's mercy, He will give you another chance. He will give you an Elijah to whom you can align eyeball to eyeball so that you can receive the anointing of the Father.

Second Kings 2:9-10 tells how Elisha cried out to Elijah and asked that he might receive Elijah's anointing when Elijah died. Elijah answered, *"If you see me when I am taken from you, it will be yours—otherwise not."*[6] What did Elijah mean when he said, "If you see me"? What if it was in the middle of the night? What if Elisha happened to blink and miss it, or if he was in the tent changing his clothes?

My friend, Dr. Mark Hanby, teaches that in the original language Elijah's response to Elisha was actually an idiom. It was a grammatical expression. Elijah was saying, "If you have allowed me to teach, train, and instruct you, then whenever I die, what is in me will automatically flow into you. Your open heart and willingness to be taught will posture you to receive what I have to give you."

Fathers are people who will not just tell you what to do but will also walk with you and care for you while they are giving you the truth. The issue is not having more teachers or better Bible studies. The issue is having fathers, and fathers who care for the anointing and passion of the Lord Jesus that dwells within you.

As I meditated on this chapter, I asked myself, "Do I really want my children to imitate me? Do I really want them to follow in my footsteps and act the way I act? All our children haven't grown up yet. Do I have the right to make such statements?" I am a man who is painfully aware of his human frailty, but with all the strength that is within me and without any apologies, I say to my sons and other children in the faith, "Follow me. Do what I do. Live like I live."

Turn *the* Hearts of the *Fathers*

Malachi 4:6 is a Scripture that has fascinated me: "[In the last days] *He will turn the hearts of the fathers to the children, and the hearts of the children to their fathers....*" As I looked at that verse 20 years ago, I was puzzled by it. The big term back then was "the generation gap." I perceived that Malachi was saying, "In the last days, God will close the generation gap."

When God turns the hearts of the fathers to the children and the children to the fathers, there will be an enveloping of the Spirit of God. There will be such a sense of co-labor and care that, although we are at different stages in our lives, we are one in Christ. As a temple of the Holy Ghost, every person requires the same level of respect and care as anyone else. Regard no one according to the flesh.[7] Don't look at people according to how old they are or how big they are on the outside. Recognize that children are spiritual beings with a great capacity to know God. Far from diminishing their importance, Jesus exhorted us to be like them![8]

This perspective is foundational to the restoration of the generations because it eliminates the whole issue of separating people according to their ages. We really need to move beyond the traditional Western concept of the Church. We are so focused on training adults, finding their gifts, and bringing them into their ministries, that we don't even think about training children. Children spend week after week in Sunday schools that are primarily baby-sitting services until children reach the age when we think that they can understand spiritual truths. We read Bible stories to them until they hit the teen years. Only then do we begin to talk to them about their purpose, destiny, and ministry. By the time a child is a teenager, it is much more difficult to bring him into God's plan for his life.

Fathering THE NEXT GENERATION

The world's systems understand the importance of training children. Socialist and Communist countries know what they want their children to be when they are adults. They begin teaching children when they are in kindergarten so that by the time those children are teenagers, the particular ideology that has been imparted is an absolute way of life.

The American culture also trains children. Our nation is far too sophisticated to call it brainwashing, but nonetheless, from the time our children are very young they are indoctrinated. Social and secular humanism are firmly implanted, and children grow up believing the lies of an anti-Christ culture.

Children *do* need their minds renewed, redirected, and changed. Many of our sons and daughters are in secular schools five days a week. They are exposed to a myriad of educational and cultural pressures. Our children are surrounded by books, games, and movies that present values that oppose what we want for them. Beginning at a young age, we must pour the Word of the Lord into our children and implant in them our spiritual culture.[9] We must saturate their very beings with the fact that they have a destiny; God has dreamed a dream for their lives.

CHILDREN *Naturally* IMITATE

Go beyond just teaching Bible verses; demonstrate and *live* the Word of God in front of your sons and daughters every day. That is what becomes the indelible mark in the heart of a child. They will automatically do things the way you do them. The more that you are loved and respected by your children, the more they will automatically act the way you act.

Not only parents, but the church family as a whole must strengthen the bonds between them and the boys and girls in their lives. It is the very anointing of God that passes through us into children. When we begin to understand and implement the things I've spoken about in this book, we will hold the importance of training children in a much higher place of value.

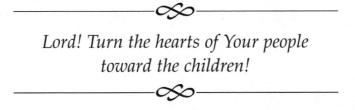

*Lord! Turn the hearts of Your people
toward the children!*

We have a big job ahead of us, don't we? But God has given us the tools to accomplish the task. I urge you to submit yourselves to the Lord and not despise the discipline. Do not despise the discipleship process that will make you, and the generations to follow you, the kind of people who can boldly say:

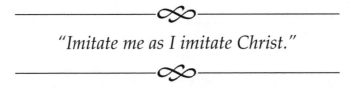

"Imitate me as I imitate Christ."

ENDNOTES

1. See 1 Timothy 1:15-16 NASB.
2. See 1 Corinthians 15:9 NKJV.
3. See 2 Corinthians 5:16 NKJV.
4. See 1 Corinthians 4:15 NKJV.
5. See Psalm 119:59.
6. 2 Kings 2:9b.
7. See 2 Corinthians 5:16 NASB.
8. See Matthew 18:3.
9. See Ephesians 5:26; Titus 3:5.

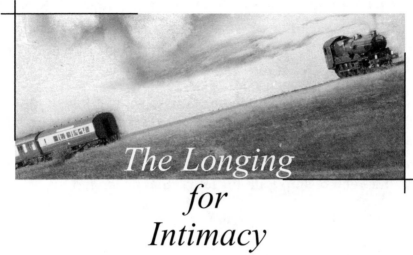

CHAPTER THIRTEEN

The Longing for Intimacy

My father loved me, and he demonstrated that love. He used to say, "I don't care if you are 35 years old. I don't care if your friends are around or not. Every time I see you, I'm going to throw my arms around you, give you a kiss on the cheek, and tell you I love you!"

Years later, when I was married with a family of my own, I remember one weekend when my parents came to visit. A friend of mine, who owned a painting business, was helping me put a new roof on our house. We were in my front yard getting some material ready when my parents drove up. I gave Mom a big hug while Dad talked to Kim. Mom went into the house and I turned to hug my father. To my surprise, Dad hesitated, looked over at Kim, and reached out to shake my hand. "What's *this*?!" I asked. I brushed his hand aside, hugged his neck, kissed his cheek, and told him I loved him.

You would have thought my dad had won a million dollars. I can still see the expression on his face. About six months later my father died, and I am so thankful to have that memory. As I watched Dad go into the house, I recall thinking that he walked a little taller than he had a few moments earlier. I turned to get back to work, and there was my friend, that big, burly painter was standing in the middle of the yard with tears streaming down his face.

What happened that day did more to show my love for the Lord than a hundred Bible studies would have done. Kim had seen something demonstrated that he himself wanted. My friend had a loving wife and three great children, but he didn't have the relationship with his father that he longed for.

The *Longing* for Intimacy in *Teens*

When children grow up with a close friendship with their parents, they don't feel the need to go outside the home to find the intimacy their hearts yearn for. Every human being needs gratification. We are not "neutral" people. We need closeness and intimacy. Young people need daily demonstration and daily verbalization of love. They need daily hugs, kisses, and words of encouragement from their parents. If unmet, the longing for intimacy turns into frustration, and teens will often seek fulfillment through sexual means. They will seek gratification from wherever they can get it.

There is a gaping chasm within every person that demands to be filled. Loving human relationships prepare a child's heart for closeness with Father God. He is the only One who can really fulfill the desperate inner longing of our hearts. Where there is no spiritual reality, we all tend to seek natural fulfillment.

If we do not present children with a living God, we cannot expect them to stay away from the only alternative. Their passions and desires need to be fulfilled. They will be satisfied either through a dynamic friendship with the living God, or through the earthly gratification of fleshly desire. Our choice has been to try to keep them from both. It is as though we want them to be locked in neutral. By doing this we are forcing them to live an existence that is totally alien to who we are as a species. We tell young people to stay away from sin or they will burn in hell, but we don't give them a relationship with the living God. We make them live in a state of neutral nothingness. They *cannot* live that way, so there will be rebellion. There will be a push toward gratification of one kind or another.

FATHER TO *Son*

As our sons reached their teenage years, I took each one aside and talked very seriously about purity and holiness in their bodies. As I talked, I saw that it was a non-issue to them. They had already determined to keep themselves pure.

When our two oldest sons were dating their prospective wives, I again took them aside and talked even more seriously. Again, it was a non-issue. In both instances our sons had already made a covenant with their fiancées to keep their relationships pure. This is not to say that I didn't need to talk to them. Our conversation reinforced, both to them and to me, that we shared the same convictions regarding sexual purity. It also reinforced to them that I wasn't assuming anything. I cared and I was watching.

Reversing PEER PRESSURE

If there is an establishment of the Presence and power of God in the hearts of young people, they will be spared the agony, grief, and ridicule of peer pressure that can be so prevalent through the teenage years. If our sons and daughters feel loved and accepted by us, and if they have real live heroes to spend time with, the need for acceptance by their peers will be greatly diminished. We told our sons that they had two choices: "You can give into the peer pressure, acting like the people you want as friends. Or you can stand firm in who you are and reverse the peer pressure. Be a leader, not a follower. Make people want to be like you!"

In our son Matt's senior year at high school, the other kids nicknamed him "the walking Hallmark card." Matthew hadn't succumbed to the pressure of being just part of the crowd. He stayed true to who he is, a genuinely caring and encouraging person. He spent countless evenings and weekends pouring into the lives of his classmates, being a real friend who was always there for them, always telling them the truth.

To *Look* Like Jesus

Our purpose is to prepare and release our sons and daughters into the purposes of God, whatever those purposes might be. We want a generation of young people so filled up with God that they will do what He wants them to do. They will pass on their fire to the generations that will follow. Our children will go where we have been too religious to go. They will talk to people whom we are too afraid to talk to. Their journey with the Lord will far exceed our own.

Our children are individuals. We cannot (and should not try to) control what God is doing in them any more than we can control what kind of plant comes up out of the ground. Our responsibility is to nurture, water, and weed so that the plant can reach its full potential. Our children are not clones. They will not grow up to look like us, or like their siblings. Our job is to fill them with a relationship with Jesus, the Word of God,[1] and to help them grow up to look as much as possible like Jesus.

God's Word will not return void.[2] If we pour the Word of God in, we will get the Word of God out—but the Word is a living Person. How much of what we teach young people is actually the living Word, and how much is nothing more than religious legalism? When we train young people in the Word, we must understand that it is not just the Bible study but also *the life of the one who gives the Bible study* that will endure. *Who we are* has more of a lasting impact than what we say to children. Who we are is what they will remember over time, for it is who we are that will impact our children. It's not what we say that has lasting power. When Christ, the living Word, dwells powerfully within us, we will impart Him.

ENDNOTES

1. See John 1:1-4.
2. See Isaiah 55:11 KJV.

CHAPTER FOURTEEN

Who Cares
About
Tomorrow?

The Kingdom of God is a living thing. It is not a gift or a castle or a building that is willed from one generation to the next. Its ownership is not loaned, leased, or sold. The Kingdom of God is a living thing that resides in us and will be transferred to living people in the next generation.

God wants us to love and care for children—not just our own, but all children. Let's not think that the Kingdom will be established on earth just by our going door-to-door handing out gospel tracts. (You know, people who hand out tracts rarely get phone calls in difficult times. People who give of themselves are the ones who get the phone calls.) Let's not deceive ourselves to think we can put the anointing into books, tapes, or seminar notes. Those things will help ignite another generation, but they won't pass on the torch of His Presence.

It is not our duty to stuff our children with our traditions and teach them how to have "church." It is our responsibility to teach our sons and daughters to hear from God. They are the Church—all the time. The Lord is unlikely to move the way you and I expect Him to. He has a plan, and our children need to be taught to hear the voice of the Lord and to obey that voice for their generation as we have had to hear His voice for our generation.

We are parenting children who are destined to be deliverers. By the mercy of God we have the opportunity to train and impact a "chosen generation."[1] Who knows but that it may be the sound of our own children's voices who will one day cry out to the heavens and say, "The kingdoms of this earth have become the Kingdom of our Lord and of His Christ."[2]

Jesus Christ, the "Ancient of Days," is on a mission. Through His death, burial, and resurrection, His shed blood holds the power to break generational sin so that you and your children can walk in obedience to Him. When Jesus died on the Cross, He prepared for us far more than most people have ever experienced. Most of us live just touching the fringe of His garment[3]—in stark comparison to those who will embrace Him in loving, determined obedience.

For some of you, your purpose and destiny may seem to be elusive, like sand passing through your fingers. How are you ever going to get a hold on it? Destiny and purpose in your *life* begin with a personal commitment to establish His Presence in your *heart*.

You can't even begin to think about passing something on to the next generation until something is established in you. When you are willing to allow God's purposes to rule your life, the Holy Spirit is able to talk to you and give you direction. Spiritual maturity begins when He tells you to do something and you do it—without grumbling, complaining, or murmuring. Possessing your destiny begins when God speaks to your heart, and you take a deep breath and say "okay."

Begin to take charge of your own life in Christ and say, "I am responsible. It's not my spouse. It's not my boss. It's not that old leaking sanctuary we meet in. It's not the government's problem. I'm not blaming anybody else. It's not even the devil's fault because he's defeated. It's my problem. It's time for me to get serious with God and His plan for my life."

The worst feeling in the world
would be to lay on your deathbed
knowing that you didn't accomplish
that for which you were born.

It's decision time. "Today, if you hear His voice, do not harden your hearts...."[4] There is a time for everything under Heaven.[5] Today, as the Spirit of the Lord is speaking to your heart, is the time to respond to His voice.

THE ROAD OF *Repentance*

Where are you in your journey with the Lord? Have you been walking with Him for many years, or have you even begun? Wherever you are in your relationship with God, setting out on a new road begins with repentance. It means turning away from your own wandering path to go His way.

The words I have written in this book are meant to encourage you. If any reader has reached these final pages feeling frustrated or inadequate, I want to offer you hope. I recognize that some people, knowing that the words in this book are true, may be overwhelmed. If you feel unable to do what you now know you should do, that in itself is good news. The very fact that you have that feeling in your heart means that you have the desire and the will to be who you need to be. Your prayer of repentance and total surrender to Jesus starts you back on the road that you love so dearly.

Finding THE ROAD OF *Repentance*

Perhaps you are someone who has never begun that journey. Perhaps you can't comprehend what it's like to know beyond a shadow of a doubt that you will go to Heaven when you die. Without a firm understanding of what will happen to your own soul, it is impossible for you to raise your children with a generational attitude. For you, the beginning point of implementing the truths in this book is to repent of your sin, call upon the Lord Jesus Christ, and ask Him to be the Lord of your life. Here is a prayer to help you get started in your life with Him:

> *Lord Jesus, I need You. I realize that I have lived my life apart from You, and that is not what You intended for me. You have a destiny and a plan that can be fulfilled only as I give control of my life to You. I want to do that. Today, _____(insert the date), I ask You, Jesus Christ, to forgive my sins. I ask You to come into my heart and be my Savior and my Lord. From now on, my life is not my own; I have given it to You. Help me to follow Your path every day. Give me the strength to turn away from my own desires and to seek You with all my might. May every dream You have dreamed for my life come true. Jesus, light the torch of Your Presence in my heart, amen.*

If you prayed that prayer, congratulations! You have begun a great adventure. Let me encourage you to read the Bible and pray every day. (Here are some Scriptures to read: Jeremiah 29:11-13; Romans 10:13; Isaiah 1:18; and First John 1:9.) Ask the Lord to lead you to a fellowship of believers where you will be encouraged and guided as a new Christian.

Returning TO THE ROAD OF *Repentance*

For other readers, you know that the words of this book are true. Maybe you were taught these things. Perhaps there was a time in your life when you actually lived according to the truths you have seen here. Turmoil and stress have caused you to turn away, but the fact that you are reading these words is evidence that no matter how far away you think you have gone, there is a longing to return to the path God has for your life. Finding that path is just a prayer of repentance away...

> *Jesus, forgive me. I have been going down a road that I now acknowledge was not the path You wanted me to take. Today, _____(insert the date), I ask You to forgive me for all of my wandering ways.* (List specific sins and areas where you have done what you wanted and not what He wanted.) *I want to be obedient and follow You, Lord. I want to make a difference. I want to fulfill the purpose and destiny You have for me. I want my life to count for eternity. I want the torch of Your Presence to burn in my heart, and I want to pass that Light to the children around me. I need Your help. Give me the strength and the courage to serve You the rest of my life, amen.*

(Here are some Scriptures to read: Second Chronicles 7:14; Psalm 32:5; 51:1; 103:12; Jeremiah 30:2-5; and Joel 2:13.)

FOCUS *on* THE ROAD OF *Repentance*

Some of you have been strong believers. You have walked with God but perhaps have never understood the significance of what I have dealt with in this book. Thank God; rejoice that at this point in your life, there is an awakening of your heart to understand the importance of the generations. Pray that God will give you direction. Ask Him what changes need to take place in your life so that you can refocus. Specifically ask Him: How can the children around me reap the benefits of who I am and what I have learned? Then allow the Lord to help you pour into the lives of young people so that the gifts and anointing He placed in your life will live on, and that the Kingdom of God will grow from strength to strength, and from generation to generation.

There are people who need what you have. Get rid of the hindrances in your life. Be a hero. Be a mentor who pours into others and then is thrilled to see those people excel you. Would to God that there would be a Church of mentors, heroes, and fathers who say, "I will tell you everything I know, and everything I think I know, that if by any means, you might excel in whatever God has planned for you. I will pour into your life all that God has poured into me. Carry the torch!"

ENDNOTES

1. See 1 Peter 2:9 KJV.
2. See Revelation 11:15.
3. See Matthew 9:20.
4. Hebrews 3:15b.
5. See Ecclesiastes 3:1.

Father, we commit the words on these pages to You.
I ask You to help us be willing to allow You to make
adjustments in our lives. Lord, speak to us.
Although we have tried to do so many things
for our children that You've told us to do in the past,
we see this critical dimension of the gospel that
You are adding to us. Adjust our thinking;
adjust our mind-sets and attitudes.

In Jesus' mighty name we declare,
*"**No** more sour grapes!*
No more allowing the sins of our forefathers
to influence our lives or the lives
of future generations!"

Jesus, we want You to build Your Church
and establish Your Kingdom in us and
in our children so that all You have poured
into us can be poured into a generation
yet to be born. We know that Your anointing
must reside in living people. We give ourselves
to You for preparation and for instruction,
yielding ourselves to Your purposes so that
the torch of Your glorious Presence will indeed
be passed on throughout the ages.
In Jesus' name we pray, amen.

Contact Information

DON NORI

c/o Destiny Image Publishers
167 Walnut Bottom Rd.
Shippensburg, PA 17257

Ph: 717-532-3040   **Ext: 124**

E-mail: dfn@destinyimage.com

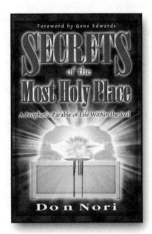

To understand where you are going, first you must know where you have been.

SECRETS OF THE
MOST HOLY PLACE VOL. 1
BY DON NORI

Here is a prophetic parable you will read again and again. The winds of God are blowing, drawing you to His Life within the Veil of the Most Holy Place. There you begin to see as you experience a depth of relationship your heart has yearned for. This book is a living, dynamic experience with God.

ISBN 1-56043-076-1

Heaven is my destination, but it is not my destiny. Many will reach their destination, but few will achieve their destiny.

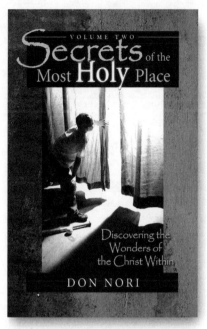

SECRETS OF THE MOST HOLY PLACE VOL. 2
BY DON NORI

Prophetic parable matures into prophetic reality as His presence draws us into the realm of 'all God.' Here, what we believe becomes what we experience and what we know becomes flesh in mere mortal man.

This book is not for the casual reader. It is for those who hunger, not for education, but for reality; not for religion, but for Him.

ISBN 0-7684-2175-6

The first steps to a life within the
Most Holy Place must be taken
into His Manifest Presence.

HIS MANIFEST PRESENCE
BY DON NORI

We must move from David's Tabernacle worship to Solomon's
Temple, where *His Manifest Presence* is experienced, if we
are to live His fullness and His protection through the tumul-
tuous days ahead. Here are some ways in which you can enter
His presence.

ISBN 0-914903-48-9

The secret to knowing God's plans and desires for your personal destiny!

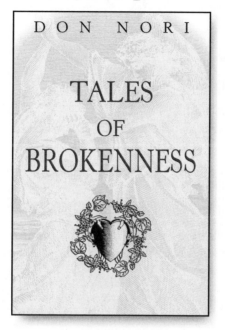

TALES OF BROKENNESS
BY DON NORI

Brokenness—the disdain of tyrants and the wonder of kings. Her mystery has eluded the intellectual and empowered the noble of heart. From her bosom flows the power and compassion to change the world.

In *Tales of Brokenness* you'll meet this companion who never forgets her need of mercy, never forgets the grace that flows on her behalf. She is the secret to knowing God's plans and desires and to finding your way to your personal destiny.

ISBN 0-7684-2074-1

A story of True Love...
and the fulfillment it brings!

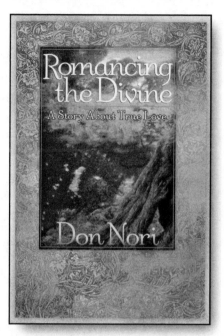

ROMANCING THE DIVINE
BY DON NORI

Romancing the Divine is a tale of every person's journey to find the reality of God. It is a tale of hope, a search for eternal love, and for all the possibilities we have always imagined would be the conclusion of such a search. In this story you will most assuredly recognize your own search for God, and discover the divine fulfillment that His love brings.

ISBN 0-7684-2053-9

Additional copies of this book and other
book titles from DESTINY IMAGE are
available at your local bookstore.

Call toll free: 1-800-722-6774.

Send a request for a catalog to:

Destiny Image® Publishers, Inc.
P.O. Box 310
Shippensburg, PA 17257-0310

*"Speaking to the Purposes of God for This
Generation and for the Generations to Come"*

**For a complete list of our titles,
visit us at www.destinyimage.com**